Penguin Masterstudies

The Miller's Tale

John E. Cunningham was educated at the Lawrence Sheriff School, Rugby, and the University of Birmingham, where, as an undergraduate and later as a research scholar, he studied under the late Professor Allardyce Nicoll. He is the author of books on the Victorian theatre and on Elizabethan and Restoration drama. He has been an Examiner in English for several of the major G.C.E. boards, and is currently Examiner in General Studies for the Oxford and Cambridge Board. He has also lectured for the Workers' Educational Association, written courses for Wolsey Hall, Oxford. and been a tutor to the Open University. He has taught English in both public and maintained schools, and is now Head of the Department of English at Varndean Sixth Form College, Brighton. He was given a complete edition of Chaucer's works in 1943 and is still trying to read it with greater understanding.

Penguin Masterstudies
Joint Advisory Editors:
Stephen Coote and Bryan Loughrey

Chaucer

The Miller's Tale

John E. Cunningham

Penguin Books

Penguin Books Ltd, Harmondsworth, Middlesex, England
Viking Penguin Inc., 40 West 23rd Street, New York, New York 10010, U.S.A.
Penguin Books Australia Ltd, Ringwood, Victoria, Australia
Penguin Books Canada Ltd, 2801 John Street, Markham, Ontario, Canada L3R 1B4
Penguin Books (N.Z.) Ltd, 182–190 Wairau Road, Auckland 10, New Zealand

Made and printed in Great Britain by
Richard Clay (The Chaucer Press) Ltd, Bungay, Suffolk
Filmset in 9/11pt Monophoto Times by
Northumberland Press Ltd, Gateshead, Tyne and Wear

The copy text used for this edition is that of the second edition of
The Complete Works of Geoffrey Chaucer, edited by Rev. W. W. Skeat,
published by Oxford at the Clarendon Press

Contents

Acknowledgements

Anyone who has been studying and trying to teach an author for forty years will have acquired a mass of information and ideas, much of which it is impossible to trace to its sources. It follows that no formal acknowledgements of scholastic debts can be paid, though the Bibliography will give some idea of the major ones. The author would like, however, to express his personal thanks to a number of people: to Bryan Loughrey, the kindly midwife to this labour; to Kenneth and Michael Grose, father and son, for debts direct and indirect; to Lower Sixth Alpha, who did not let him get away with sloppy statements; to the staff of Burgess Hill Library for patiently looking up many bizarre details; and, for help of a most practical kind, to 'myn Alisoun', Alyson Nikiteas.

J.E.C.

Introduction

Anyone who is about to study a work of literature has to bear in mind two questions. What did this mean when it was written? What does it mean now? To understand the writing of the past we have to know something of the background, the general views which the author and his first readers had, the possible changes there have been not only in the direct meaning but also in the overtones of the words he uses. If what we are studying is truly a work of art, each age will find something new in it, some reflection of itself: Shakespeare would probably be very surprised to see a modern performance of *Hamlet*, just as we should probably find an eighteenth-century version of it downright funny, and no doubt the twenty-first century will consider the play afresh and find new aspects to emphasize. The point is that each *Hamlet* has been valid in its own time.

Chaucer looks more 'difficult' than Shakespeare, and anyone about to study him – as many users of this book may be – for the first time is likely to ask two further questions. Why should I read this at all? If I must read it to satisfy some syllabus requirement, why can I not read it in a modern version? The purpose of this Introduction is to try to answer these two questions; the purpose of the whole book is to help towards an answer to the first pair – what did it mean and what does it mean to us now?

Chaucer lived from about 1340 to 1400: that is to say, he lived during a period of great changes, many of which are reflected in the stories he told and the remarkable collection of characters he assembled to tell them. At the beginning of the century in which he was born, the mass of English people worked on the land and lived in small villages. Most labourers had strips of land – you can still see the pattern of ridges and furrows in old pastureland all over England – which produced just about enough for them to live on; but they held these from their feudal overlord, and had to give him so many days' free labour on his own estates each year. They were not free to move to another district, or even to marry without his consent. That is why none of them appear on the pilgrimage to Canterbury. The only 'labourer' amongst the pilgrims is a ploughman, a skilled workman who could sell his services and probably had a little land of his own. A cut above him – at least in his own estimation – is the Miller, also a skilled workman but enjoying the privileges of a monopoly: most people had little choice in where they took their grain to be ground – again, in practice, it was often a matter of the lord on whose land you lived saying which mill you must use.

The pattern loosely called serfdom suggests a slave state to a modern reader, but the feudal system was not wholly a means for the rich to oppress the poor. True, the Church exacted a tithe or tenth of everyone's income – today the state takes about a third of ours in direct taxation, and a lot more in indirect ways, in return for the varying material provisions for our welfare which we enjoy and Chaucer's times did not. The Church offered them the only means to eternal life – and, at a somewhat lower level, a calendar containing about 165 holy days or holidays. (It was on just such a day that Alison first caught the eye of the amorous Absolon in church.) In the secular feudal world, everyone had reciprocal duties and obligations, though then as always it was easier for those in the higher levels of society to neglect their responsibilities while insisting ruthlessly on their fulfilment by those below. But this system had creaked along after a fashion since the Norman Conquest. When Chaucer was a small boy it was, as we shall see, appallingly disrupted by natural causes. When he was a middle-aged man he lived through another up-heaval, this time a social one, which one historian has called 'the most remarkable incident in our long history – the capture of London'. The second event evolved from the first. Both were to affect Chaucer's world profoundly.

The first crisis, the 'natural' one, was the Black Death, which spread throughout England in 1348–9, and remained dormant, with sporadic outbreaks in the summer and occasional very severe recurrences, until the later part of the seventeenth century. The first outbreak which swept across Europe killed perhaps a third of the population. In the words of a contemporary, 'half the world died', and that is how it must have seemed to them. It is hard to judge the effect on men's minds. Today, most of us do not believe in a vengeful God, or in Hell: we expect diseases to have ascertainable causes (we know the plague was carried by a rat-flea and vanished when the carriers were ousted by another type of rat) and we also expect illness to be either curable or at least capable of alleviation. If we try to imagine the effects of international nuclear war we may get some sense of the scale and horror of the Plague, but at least we know something about how atomic weapons work, that they are man-made, who has them – and we can, if we wish, try to prevent such devices being used. Nobody knew how the Black Death was caused or carried. Nobody was safe from it, aristocrat or peasant, priest or murderer, child or man. It embedded itself deep in the consciousness of the survivors, and re-mained in the national consciousness for generations to come. Many of

Chaucer's stories remind us that death was just around the corner – *The Pardoner's Tale*, *The Monk's Tale* and *The Knight's Tale*, for example; when he tells us that men feared the Reeve 'like the deeth' he may have meant 'like the Black Death'. Even the frivolous tale told by the Miller against that same Reeve has a tinge of this darkness within it: Nicholas plays upon the Carpenter's fear that the world is, as he calls it, 'ful tikel', an extremely chancy place, and he makes great use of an associated fear in the medieval mind, that the end of the world and the Day of Judgement might come at any moment. Every Sunday the Church reminded men of their frail grip on this mortal world. Every summer the Plague came back to reinforce the sermon.

Besides this spiritual effect there was an enormous social result of the huge death-roll. Suddenly there was a serious shortage of labour to work feudal property. Men realized that they could now escape from their villages and seek someone who would pay them for their services and not be too particular in asking whether they were freemen or not. So began, for many working men, the mobility of labour which was to give labourers themselves an inkling of their own importance and so of their power. The second upheaval we referred to above took place in 1381. In the south-eastern part of England a group of labourers who had been subjected to some very unpopular taxation gathered together, marched on London, took the Tower, executed the Archbishop of Canterbury, murdered foreign workmen such as the groups of Flemish weavers and were pacified only by the courage – and duplicity – of the teenage king, Richard II, who faced the angry mob, promised to meet all their demands, got them to disband and promptly went back on his promises.

Twice in his life, then, Chaucer must have felt that he had seen the world turned upside down. Though there are few direct references to these tremendous events in his writing – why mention what everybody knew? – we can trace an awareness of change and instability, an interest in classes that were vanishing, like the Knight, and in the rising men of the middle classes, merchants, skilled men, even millers . . .

Above all, the pilgrimage itself, which is the thread upon which all the tales are hung, is a sign of men's need for a faith in troubled times. The very mixed group of people who assemble at the Tabard are going to Canterbury to pay their dues to the martyr who had helped them 'when they were sick' – a term which covers both bodily and spiritual states. Scholars have sometimes tried to set a date for the pilgrimage as though it were a real event. This is an amusing game to play, though of no rational importance. However, the sort of date arrived at by studying internal evidence – the campaigns the Knight had been on, for instance – suggests only a few years after the Peasants' Revolt, as we have come to call it, took place.

This was an upheaval special to England. The international background to the whole of Chaucer's life, rarely mentioned no doubt because it had always been there, was the Hundred Years War. This long dynastic struggle for power in France began a few years before Chaucer was born and continued for half a century after his death. For much of his lifetime England was under an unstable government because Edward III outlived his eldest son, the Black Prince, whose tomb is still one of the glories of Canterbury, thus leaving a little grandson as nominal ruler of the country. That grandson was to gather round him a court of high fashion, much of it based on French models, and his country was the harder to rule because the earlier successes in the French wars had brought prosperity, not to say loot, to campaigners good and bad, and the prosperity of local men tends to increase national violence and unrest. Something of the turbulent state of the realm may be found in one of Chaucer's most vivid pieces of writing, the description of the Temple of Mars in *The Knight's Tale*. Chaucer had served abroad as a youth, just as the Knight had, and had seen the world of action at first hand.

At home, one other result of the prolonged war abroad was the presence of a number of French aristocratic prisoners, some of whom had to wait years for their ransoms to be paid, and who led quite relaxed lives, encouraging foreign graces, clothes, cookery, styles of courtship, all of which have their reflection in *The Tales*. It may seem a far cry from a French prisoner to *The Miller's Tale*, but Absolon's wooing is very much *à la mode*. This easy intermingling of captive and captor was helped by the fact that they had a common language – court French: yet even here another change, and a very important one, was taking place as Chaucer was growing up. Latin was, and remained until the eighteenth century, an international language for men of learning, and most serious works were written in it. When the Normans conquered England they found their new subjects spoke a variety of dialects of Old English or Anglo-Saxon – a strong, gritty, Germanic tongue with a very complex grammar. The Normans, or Northmen, were, as their name implies, Vikings who had settled in the area of France still known as Normandy. They had acquired their own way of speaking French, which they brought with them to this country, and this continued to be the language of the court and of officialdom until Chaucer's day, though it underwent modifications and became less like the French spoken in France. The native 'English' population naturally began to pick up words and phrases from their new masters, and soon many people who had to deal between the rulers and the ruled must have become bilingual. The complex grammar of Old English began to be simplified while its vocabulary extended to take in many loan-words from French – so much so that in Chaucer's lifetime two significant acts of recognition took place: English became the official language in which lawsuits were pleaded (though they were still recorded, and were for centuries later, in French – the law does not hurry itself unduly); and English became the official language of instruction in schools. There is some argument about which English king was the first to speak English as his natural tongue, but Richard II certainly spoke it and his successor, Henry IV, who ruled in the last year of Chaucer's life, seems to have made it his language of choice.

Chaucer's friend and contemporary, Gower, wrote works in English, French and Latin, and Chaucer was quite capable of doing this – probably he could have managed Italian, too – but it is of great significance that he chose to set down his very wide range of work including his technical treatise on astronomy, his prose version of a sixth-century philosopher, occasional poems, courtly romance and the immense diversity of *The Canterbury Tales* in his own English. We can call it 'his own' because he spoke a dialect, that of the East Midlands. This, which tended to become the accepted speech of the capital, was to help the movement towards the idea of a standardized form of English, a problem brought to a head a hundred years later by the introduction of printed books. Chaucer's work, of course, was meant to be read aloud from a single, expensive manuscript copy. A century later Caxton, in a famous preface to one of his new, printed books, tells us a story of how, in one part of England, the plural of the word 'egg' was 'eyren', in another it was 'eggs'. If he was to print books for a wide circulation, which was he to choose?

Despite the fact that we can now settle most problems of this sort by reference to a dictionary, it may have occurred to you that in many ways Chaucer lived through times not at all unlike our own. The present century has seen enormous changes in social structure, upheavals in conditions of labour, political unrest at home and abroad and a constant background of wars and fear of wars, including, since 5 August 1945, the possibility of the end of the world, or of our part in it. On a less sensational level, our language also has changed: there has been a vast influx of new words coined to meet our technical innovations, so much so that Chambers find it necessary to publish an entire, separate dictionary to contain them – some 60,000 of them, in fact. The mention of dictionaries may remind us of another kind of standardization that Chaucer never imagined or cared about, though Caxton had to – the idea of 'correct' spelling. The spread of radio and television means that we now share a concept of a 'correct' way of pronouncing, though, luckily, these same media also help to keep local accents alive; but an accent is not a dialect, and few genuine dialect-speakers remain – Geordie is perhaps as good an example as any of a sub-language with its own vocabulary and constructions as well as its own pronunciation.

In some ways, then, Chaucer's experience of the world may not have been so very different from ours; but differences there were, and we must consider some of them if we are to make sense of his stories.

We might begin with the activity which brings his story-tellers together. People still go on pilgrimages, but they are not a popular activity in this country. Chaucer's world was a Roman Catholic one; he believed in Heaven, Hell and Purgatory in between. Over the chancel arch of many country churches we can still see the remains of lurid paintings of the Last Judgement set there to remind the simple worshipper every Sunday of what was one day in store for everybody. The Church pervaded every corner of life then, where now it is at best peripheral and to many people wholly irrelevant. When we look at the pilgrims, it is surprising – to us – to find how many of them are in, or in some way connected with, the Church: even in the bawdy story we are to study, one of the characters is a parish clerk and another is devout enough to fear the annihilation of mankind by God at any moment. Even the student, Nicholas, is a sort of embryonic churchman, since that was the chief end of university studies. And besides the more formal aspects of the Church, there was a host of wandering preachers, friars and pardoners amongst them, who could entertain and terrify with a rousing hell-fire sermon – a reminder that an illiterate population enjoyed the act of listening in a way that it is hard for us to grasp. Where books were rare and very costly, and writing materials hard to come by, people relied on their ears and a very high degree of accurate memory-work.

If they were accurate in memory, about many things they might seem extraordinarily vague to us. Had you asked Chaucer what the date was or what time it was or how old he was or how he wrote his name, the answer would probably have surprised you as much as such questions would have surprised him. He thought of dates in terms of Church festivals and the calendar of astrology (the date of the pilgrimage is established by the position of the sun in the sign of Aries, the dates of *The Miller's Tale* are no more than days of the week); time he might think of in terms of the seven offices of the religious day, the so-called 'canonical hours' kept by monasteries and friary churches (the love-making of Alison and Nicholas continues until 'the belle of laudes gan to ringe'), or the strange system known as the 'unequal hours', dating back to Roman times, by which the day was divided into twelve sections from sunrise to sunset and the night similarly into another twelve, so that, except at the equinoxes, the hours were never of the same length in darkness as they were in daylight. So the time-scheme of most of his stories seems remarkably vague to us, though it would have been clear and adequate to his contemporaries.

To revert to our imaginary questions, he wrote his name as he pleased, and if he kept to one spelling it would have been because it was easy to write or looked stylish. It is on record that, on one occasion, being asked formally to give his age in a legal matter he said that he was 'over forty' and that was probably how he thought about it. The date of his birth would never have been recorded in any official way, though that of his baptism might have been – we know neither this, nor, for certain, the date of his death. A keen astronomer-astrologer – to him there was no difference – he knew that of course the planets, of which there were seven to his knowledge – the Moon, Mercury, Venus, the Sun, Mars, Jupiter and Saturn – revolved round the solid globe of the earth on which he stood, just as described by the great astronomer of second-century Alexandria, Ptolemy, whose famous book, the *Almagest*, appears in the bedroom of Nicholas, the 'hero' of *The Miller's Tale*. Earth was the centre of the whole Universe since it contained God's greatest creation.

As we have seen, the social hierarchy of the day may have been in a state of change, but to him its distinctions were perfectly clear. The famous question 'Who does he think he is?' could hardly have been asked in the fourteenth century, for it would have had no meaning. Everyone knew who he was in the social order, though of course some aspired to better themselves. On the whole, however, Chaucer would have expected the future, if he thought much about it, not to exhibit very much change: the past – which he wrote about a great deal – he would not have seen as very different from the present. Since he believed that people did not change in any fundamental way, he did not much trouble himself with historical perspective, and wrote about the past, much as Shakespeare was to do in his 'Roman' plays with their doublets and billiards and chiming clocks, as if it were the present.

We, however, have been approaching him with rather different assumptions, and perhaps we have now gone far enough, in this brief introduction, to be able to consider again the two questions we posed at the beginning: why should we read him at all, and why should we read him in the original language?

If we have any interest whatsoever in the language and literature of our own country, we must read some Chaucer, because he lived at a time which was vital to the development of both. English – still different, in many ways, as we shall see, from ours, but recognizably English – was developing quickly, both as a language and as an accepted means of expression, thought and record on a wide variety of topics. The form of English which he wrote was to set the pattern for the form of English which was to become standard. His proficiency in other languages has been mentioned. As we shall discover, he used the techniques of French and Italian in the way in which he constructed his poetry, rather than the quite different systems used in Old English, and he was the first major writer to combine the English language with European forms of stanza and metre.

As we have seen, the times he lived in bear some comparison to our own. One of the differences we have noted is that in his day the enjoyment of literature was largely aural, books being, like literacy, rare. The soul of poetry is its sound, together with the associations which words carry with them, beyond their mere dictionary definitions. We cannot hope to understand this remarkable author fully, still less to enjoy him, unless we can get at the sense that his word conveyed to his original hearers, so we must study his language; and, though this is more difficult, it is also possible to learn how to 'hear' him as we read, to hear the extraordinary and powerful mixture of sounds that emerge from the welding together of two languages of very different origins. How we may do this is dealt with later on. Here it is enough to say that a bland, modern 'translation' may be pleasant and easy to read, but it will never do more then give us the general sense of what he wrote – and this is nowhere more true than in tales of vigorous impropriety, such as the one we are now concerned to study. Our bland, modern pronunciation takes all the grit and guts out of the language – can you imagine someone telling a story, perhaps an outrageously improper one, from Scotland or Ireland, in a Standard English accent? This is the ruinous effect of turning Chaucer into 'modern' English.

One writer, perhaps over-fond of turning a good phrase, said that Chaucer 'invented the English language'. This is not a wholly extravagant claim, since his effect on it was very great. If we are to begin to study what we like to call our heritage, this is as good a place to start as we could find. *The General Prologue*, with its vivid gallery of medieval people, is immediately followed by two tales which are in high contrast yet complement one another perfectly – the elegant, chivalric love-story told by the Knight and the robust tale of sexual mayhem vigorously delivered by the tipsy Miller. The first three sections of *The Canterbury Tales* form a fitting gateway through which we may follow his many other readers, adaptors, translators and admirers, of whom Shakespeare, Dryden and Scott are but a few of the diverse throng.

1. Chaucer's Life

For the convenience of someone coming to Chaucer's work for the first time, we give here a simple account of some of the main facts of his life, together with a comment on aspects of it which are of particular relevance in studying his writing. Much fuller treatments of his life are, of course, available, and those who are interested to pursue this further will find suggestions in the Bibliography.

Chaucer was born about 1343. Father and grandfather were both Londoners, though the latter came from Ipswich. His father, John Chaucer, was a citizen, a term which then carried some real sense of status, and dealt in wine. Chaucer shows some knowledge of the wine trade, including its tricks, in several of his writings – and of drunkenness, too: the Miller is heavily under the influence when he begins his story.

At the time of the poet's birth, John Chaucer, through connections with the court of Edward III, was able to secure some favours there; and in due course his son became a page to the wife of one of the royal dukes, Clarence. By the age of nineteen, the young man was serving as a squire with the royal forces in France, where he was captured and his ransom was paid by the king himself.

About eight years later, in 1369, he was granted a life-pension by the monarch in recognition of his services in the royal household. This was for a little more than thirteen pounds a year. It is impossible to suggest a modern equivalent, but it has been said that a country parson at that time would consider he had a comfortable living if his annual income was ten pounds.

One of Chaucer's first substantial poems was a reflection of his royal connections. In an outbreak of plague in 1369, John of Gaunt's first wife died, and Chaucer composed a work in her memory, *The Book of the Duchess*. Lionel, the Duke of Clarence, had died in the previous year, and Chaucer's services seem then to have been largely transferred to his brother, John of Gaunt, Duke of Lancaster. In the next few years he was certainly busy at court and also engaged in some diplomatic activity. Perhaps the most important aspect of this, for us, is his being sent to Italy at the end of 1372, where he remained for a year and became familiar with the literature of that country, as well as fulfilling his official mission so well that he returned to a life of increasing prosperity. He was given an important office in the Port of London, a daily ration of wine and a life-pension from Lancaster, and was able to lease a house in Aldgate. His ties with the Lancastrian house were probably increased by his marriage to Philippa, since there is reason to believe that she was the sister to the lady who became Gaunt's mistress, and, later, his third wife.

The pattern of the next few years is one of steady prosperity and favour. He received a number of gifts and offices, went to Flanders in 1377 on a secret mission, to France and Italy again the following year and was given an additional post in the Customs in 1382. Three years later, possibly again through royal favour, he was allowed to continue to hold his offices but appoint someone else to carry them out – given, in fact, a sinecure. In 1386 he was appointed Knight of the Shire for Kent – that is he represented Kent in the Parliament when the Commons were summoned to attend.

Perhaps this marked the zenith of his fortunes. We have seen already that he lived in a troubled century, and there was a long struggle for power amongst the surviving sons of Edward III, which his young grandson, Richard II, had great difficulty in controlling. It was in one of these abrupt shifts of influence, when Gaunt was out of the country – he left for Spain in the summer of 1386 – that Chaucer seems to have fallen from favour. He lost his various offices and was in such financial straits that he had to raise money on his pensions, rather as we might now raise cash on insurance policies. His wife died in the following year; but there was an ironic twist in store in 1389, when a new shift of power brought Gaunt back into prominence and Chaucer was appointed Clerk of the King's Works at a salary of nearly £40 a year, an important post entailing responsibility for the upkeep of royal buildings. In the following year he was appointed to a similar post of responsibility for St George's Chapel, Windsor, and there were other commissions related to this as well. However, life continued to be erratic. He gave up his chief post in 1391, perhaps because he had suffered robbery and assault while carrying out his duties, which might have become increasingly difficult with his advancing years (fifty was a ripe age then, we must remember), and he was to enjoy another sinecure when he became sole forester of North Petherton Park in 1398. At this period there are nevertheless indications that he was short of money – he was sued for a quite modest debt, for example.

The year 1399 was an important one for England, as it was then that the cousin of Richard II, Henry of Bolingbroke, took the throne from the increasingly ineffectual king. This was to be the beginning of a long struggle for power between the houses of York and Lancaster, and caused several uprisings, since Henry IV, the title Bolingbroke took, was not in line for the throne, being the son of a younger son. Richard died – or was murdered – childless, and the Duke of Clarence, to whose issue the crown should have gone, left no male heir. It took nearly a century for this struggle to be resolved by the accession of Henry Tudor as Henry VII after the Battle of Bosworth, which, in 1485, ended what is generally known as the Wars of the Roses.

Chaucer was concerned with more immediate problems. He wrote a poem to the new king, Henry IV, lamenting the state of his own purse, and Henry granted him a good pension, which may have encouraged him to take out a long lease on a house in Westminster. For a man of his age in those times this was an optimistic act. He died the following year and is buried in the Abbey. His grave was to form the nucleus of what is now called Poets' Corner there, and some very odd company he keeps, a fact which he might find both interesting and amusing.

Not much is known for certain of his family. He had a son – little Lewis, or Louis, as he called him in the book he wrote explaining the use of the astrolabe to the boy – but he seems to have died young. If the direct line died with him, we need not feel surprised. Such extinction was common enough. Until the late nineteenth century started to make real advances in medicine, man had little power to cure illnesses now regarded as trivial but formerly often fatal.

So far we have been looking largely at a string of facts and figures, and different commentators have put quite different interpretations on them. For example Chaucer has been seen as a middle-class boy who made good, as the product of royal patronage, as a good civil servant, as a 'European' (an expression he would not have understood), as an astute opportunist and, for quite different reasons, as an unhappily married man. It is worth spending a few moments looking at some of these assertions to see if they have any validity and also if they can help us to understand his poetry any better.

The assumption that he was unhappily married is based upon the silliest of evidence: no references to his wife survive, and in his stories – *The Miller's Tale* is a good example – he tells often of unfaithful wives. If a man is happily married he is not always referring to the fact, and probably feels more keenly the situation of those who do not share his good fortune, so the 'evidence' can be used to prove the contrary at our pleasure. As to patronage, it was the usual way to get on in the world then, and remained so until at least the beginning of the present century. He was fortunate in having more than one connection with the court. He was obviously a man who could be trusted, being sent abroad several times on diplomatic missions, and he had served as a page in a royal retinue, and as a young soldier, besides the more dignified offices of his later years.

What is beyond argument about this picture is that he had seen a lot of life – aristocratic, bureaucratic, military, diplomatic – and, as Clerk of Works, he must have had a good deal to do with tradesmen, skilled labourers and probably a fair selection of crooks, as well as suffering personal assault (the Miller is a skilled workman, a crook and a physically dangerous man). So in his travels and his duties he brushed shoulders with all sorts and conditions of men. Luckily for us he was observant, and his success in life never made him a snob. In his writing he looks upon people of almost every rank with an impartial eye – social snobbery he found amusing, and he satirizes it quietly in his picture of the aristocratic Prioress, more openly in his picture of the Miller, the Miller's wife (a priest's bastard who gave herself airs) and their attitude to their daughter – a picture given to us by the Reeve when he begins his story in revenge for the tale the Miller has just aimed at him.

As to his being a 'European' – a term which did not exist then in our sense, the world being for him divided into Christian and heathen – he had a good knowledge of French and French culture from the English court before he went to its country of origin. His visit to Italy certainly impressed him, for there he made himself acquainted with the work of Boccaccio and probably Dante, who, like Chaucer, had taken the major step of deciding to write a major poem in his own, ordinary speech, not in Latin. Equally, Chaucer seems to have benefited by his travels in other parts – the version of a well-known story which he used for the Miller to tell seems to have been Flemish, and he knew Flanders; and his knowledge of French literature went well beyond that of polite court writing, since he was familiar with, and impressed by, the *fabliaux* of which this tale is an example amongst many.

But a wide interest and a fluent command of languages does not make a man a cosmopolitan, and there were vast regions of Europe quite unknown to him personally – in one way he seems to have had a rather parochial mind, for he regarded a large part of his own country as being wild and strange. His Shipman comes from the West Country, and Chaucer says of him, 'For all I know he came from Dartmouth', rather as we might say, 'He's South American – maybe Bolivian.' He speaks of the north of England as if it were a territory of unknown barbarians, an attitude not wholly unknown in the south-east to this day. Possibly he may have found this amusing in his fellow-Londoners, for he may well have visited the northern estates of his royal master as a young man, and he knew and used well the wit and dialect of the north in the story which the Reeve tells in retaliation against the Miller. But both tales are set in the university towns of Oxford and Cambridge – he seems to know

Cambridge rather better, but *The Miller's Tale* conveys a good sense of the way Oxford probably then was – and we feel that here he is more at home than 'Far in the North, I cannot tell you where . . .'

Undeniably his travels affected his work. Though he chose to write in English, he did so in the metres and verse-patterns of Francy and Italy. If all his pilgrims are English, they often tell stories set in other countries, and he shows local knowledge of Brittany in *The Franklyn's Tale* and Italy in *The Clerk's Tale*.

This is a suitable moment to remind ourselves that, though he is best known by *The Canterbury Tales*, he was a man of astonishing output – astonishing, that is, if we consider how busy he was in worldly affairs, and how slow the process of writing then was, even if work was dictated. Not only the bulk of this work, but its range must impress us. He translated a courtly allegory, the *Romaunt of the Rose*, and a long philosophical work, the former from French, the latter from Latin; he wrote what many people would call the first English novel, the story of Troilus and Cressida, told in a highly elaborate and tricky verse-form. He wrote a handbook on the use of an astronomical instrument, the astrolabe, for his eleven-year-old son, an extremely difficult thing to do in the laboured prose of the time, which was quite unsuited to technical writing. He also left a number of short poems, some of them very fine, which give us some insights into his own feelings and experience. And the tales for which he is best known give us the whole spectrum of story-telling, from the elegant little saint's life told by the Prioress to the outrageous bawdiness of the work we are about to study here.

If there is indeed a key to unlock the life of a man at all, in Chaucer's case it might be found in one of the translations referred to above. Boethius' *Consolations of Philosophy* was written by an Italian of the sixth century while he was in prison waiting for death. It deals with the ups and downs of man's life, his ways of coping with triumph and disaster. Chaucer's life exhibits a pattern of good times and bad, sometimes with quite sudden changes, always, it seems, depending upon the goodwill or caprice of others more powerful than he. He had, we can surely say with confidence, a good understanding of the transitory nature of our change-able world, and the image of the Wheel of Fortune – 'Now up, now down, as bucket in a well' – that is central to the first of the tales is no mere rhetorical figure. He knew well that life is lived – or was in his time – in a perpetual state of unstable equilibrium, and this he learned to accept with quiet humility; even, in some of its manifestations, with amusement, as we shall see in the erratic fortunes of Nicholas and Absolon, John the Carpenter and Alison.

Our own age is so vainly conscious of its technical achievement that it tends to regard mortality itself as just another illness for which there must be a cure, and that finding it is merely a matter of time. Chaucer had more sense than to think there was a cure for death or misfortune. Nowhere in his writing does he show any fear of the former; the latter he seems to have faced with an enviable calmness.

2. The Framework and Origins of the Tales

The Miller's Tale is best understood if it is read in context, that is if we can see it as a part of a large design. In this short chapter we shall try to see the overall shape of *The Canterbury Tales*, to get some idea of Chaucer's sources, and, in particular, to say something about the place and origin of the story we are to study.

All students of Chaucer, whether they are studying him for their own interest or for an examination, ought to read *The General Prologue* to the tales, even if in a modern version. It is a fascinating portrait-gallery of the fourteenth century in itself, and also shows us what a skilful narrator Chaucer was. He intended to compile an anthology of medieval stories covering a very wide range of topics. All such collections present the same problem – how is the writer to make them cohere? Chaucer certainly knew of one such collection which is still famous, though chiefly for its reputation as a saucy book, *The Decameron*, or Ten Days' Entertainment, of the Italian writer Boccaccio. His method of stringing the stories together was very ingenious and simple – a group of ten young Florentine aristocrats, men and women, take a villa in the country to avoid an outbreak of plague in the city. They propose to pass the time telling stories, appointing a judge for each day, and a topic. The plague conveniently abates after ten days, when they return to Florence. Upon this thread are strung one hundred tales. Reading Boccacio, however, is quite different from reading Chaucer – a good, quick test is to read the Sixth Tale of Day Nine, which is basically the same as the story the Reeve tells in answer to the Miller's attack on him. All the tellers are aristocrats, so there is little variation in tone between one story and another, though there is a wide range of subject-matter; and it is rather tedious to read ten tales in a row all on exactly the same topic.

Chaucer's method allows of much greater flexibility. One of the very few occasions in medieval times when almost all ranks of men mixed and talked together fairly freely was on pilgrimage. The only exclusions were the serfs, who were tied to the land, and the highest aristocrats, who would go in their own retinue; to some extent, women would also be poorly represented – especially those who were not married. Thus the pilgrimage provides a very promising social mixture, and tales of different kinds can be told by different characters in different styles.

Instead of a judge for a day, these story-tellers have a forceful guide and arbiter for the whole journey, the Host of the Tabard Inn in South-wark, where they assembled on the night before they set out to Canterbury, probably with the idea of being early on a road that was busy by the standards of the day. The Host puts to them the notion that they should all tell two stories on the way to Canterbury and two on the way back – and he will ride with them, free of charge as he astutely mentions, and judge who tells the best story of all. The winner is to have a feast paid for by all of them when they get back to the Tabard. Thus the Host ensures that his customers will return for at least one night and pay for special entertainment. He adds a further caution, that if anyone challenges his judgement, the offender is to pay the travelling expenses of the whole company. As this is about thirty people – Chaucer was as vague about this as he usually was in mathematical matters – it would be a considera-tion of some weight.

Had the scheme been completed, we should have a hundred and twenty stories: including those which are incomplete, we have barely two dozen. A number of pilgrims are mute, and nobody tells more than one story, except Chaucer himself, who starts a jingling rhyme so awful that the Host stops him, and Chaucer meekly tells another story – a long, boring tale in prose – apologizing for his lack of narrative art.

What the author did manage to do was to block out several groups of tales, including the opening and closing series, and it is to the former that *The Miller's Tale* belongs. This is further discussed in the section dealing with the Miller himself, and also in the introductory notes to the text (see pages 38 and 41), so it is sufficient to mention here that the story-telling is opened by the man of highest rank, the Knight, who just happens to pick the shortest straw when the Host offers them all the chance to draw; and that the Knight tells a courtly romance of two men in love with the same lady, one of whom wins her after many hardships and over two thousand lines of narration of a rather lofty kind. The Miller's drunken insistence that he goes next is a neat touch of artistry – his story is at once a contrast and a complement to the first, since it is thoroughly scandalous in nature and language, yet it also is about two young men and a girl, and the ultimate success of one of them. The story is apparently aimed at the elderly Reeve, who was once a carpenter like the duped husband in the Miller's narrative, so the Reeve retaliates with a tale about a brutal Miller. That these stories form a group is quite clear, as there are connecting passages between each tale and the next.

Similar groups have been worked out by similar means, and the order in which they are printed in complete editions is usually that established by the great Chaucerian scholar, Walter Skeat, whose version of the text is used in this book. It is generally believed that Chaucer intended to arrange his stories at least partly according to themes – there is the so-called 'marriage group' for example, and probably he envisaged others dealing with stories of saints as well as of very unsaintly people such as those in the tale we are considering. He knew where he was going, at any rate, for he completed the tale that was to stand last, and wrote a short but moving epilogue to it, asking to be forgiven for all his more profane writing. The conclusion was to be the sermon preached by the poor country Parson, the most wholly virtuous representative amongst the pilgrims of a somewhat corrupt Church. It has been suggested that this is more than conventional piety, but was part of a symbolic design: the pilgrims were riding from the (sinful) city of man to the holy shrine of Canterbury, and it is right that the last story told should be telling us all how to attain grace by avoiding those sins which destroy the immortal soul. Though the last story would, in theory, have to be told on the return journey, the notion is still an attractive one.

After this analysis of the Seven Deadly Sins – for that is what the Parson takes for his subject – there is the prayer for pardon already mentioned, in which Chaucer asks us to pray for him that Christ may have mercy on him for his 'endytinges of worldly vanitees ... and the tales of Caunterbury, thilke that sounen in-to sinne'. What were the sources upon which he drew for his tales, many of which did not, of course, 'tend towards sin'? In particular, what was his source for *The Miller's Tale*?

One of the major differences between the Middle Ages and our world may well be in our attitude towards originality: we value it, they distrusted it as 'new-fangelnesse', a foolish craving for novelty. If a thing was old, it was good. If an argument was to be found in Aristotle, it was better than one in Gower, because it was older – had, in fact, that 'authoritee' which our world despises as mere clinging to the past. So Chaucer's readers would not be expecting to hear a lot of new stories, but rather familiar tales well told, and that is what he gave them.

His sources are many, and scholars would disagree often on the exact provenance of a tale. Some are obvious – there were standard books of the legends of saints upon which he could draw; well-known authors of antiquity, such as Ovid, or more recent Italian writers such as Petrarch or Boccaccio, provided ready-made plots – though some of these were drawn from a much older source, folk-stories and folk-lore. *The Miller's Tale*, like the stories told by the Sailor, the Friar and the Summoner, has its origin in the *fabliaux*. These – the name means 'little fables' – were, you will not be surprised to learn, French in origin. They were jingly rhymes, usually couplets with eight syllables to a line –

His fader was a man ful free,
And lord he was of that contree

– which sound frivolous to the ear, and generally were. They were produced quite extensively in France in the twelfth century and later, were
generally of a satirical or scandalous nature, and dealt with the goings-
on of the lower bourgeoisie and working classes. There are very few
versions in English, and Chaucer is unusual in drawing so extensively on
them as he did – perhaps because they fit in so well with his conception
of a wide social range amongst his narrators. In general it is the low-bred
folk, like the Miller, who tell such 'cherles tales'.

If they are little known in English, they were certainly popular on the
continent, and *The Miller's Tale* offers good evidence of this. Exactly
what version Chaucer used is a matter for more abstruse academic debate
than is appropriate here, though any interested reader can find an excellent analysis of it in a text referred to in the Bibliography. It is enough
here to mention three points only: the story was widely known and has
been traced in a variety of languages; the version which seems the
favourite as Chaucer's starting-point is a Flemish one; and he vastly
improved on the original.

The basic story is of a woman entertaining a series of lovers, the first
being disconcerted by the arrival of a second, and hiding, perhaps nod-
ding off in a corner like the Carpenter. Another visitor, sometimes a priest
– many of these stories were anti-clerical – is smitten with guilt, and starts
talking loudly about God's punishment of sinners, with some reference
to the Flood, which strikes the ear of the concealed lover and leads to
various forms of mishap. A third candidate for a night's pleasure is a
smith, who, rejected with insult, plans to get his own back by using a hot
piece of iron from his smithy.

It can be seen at once that Chaucer has turned a rather crude little tale
into something skilfully constructed and quite brilliantly developed, even
if some of the subject-matter is thoroughly bawdy. It will be our concern,
in the detailed study of the text which is the core of this book, to see with
what mastery he has developed both plot and characterization, without
losing the down-to-earth quality that characterized the *fabliaux* for which
he seemed to have had a genuine respect.

3. How to Read Chaucer

Before we turn from considering the general outline of *The Tales* to the Miller himself and what he has to say to us, there is one more problem to be tackled. Most users of this book will be working under professional guidance or instruction. There is no printed substitute for personal contact in study, where any difficulty or obscurity can be referred directly to the teacher, and any error in one's own understanding will be noticed and put right. No collection of notes, however exhaustive, can hope to cover the problems of every student. On the other hand, there is no substitute for working at a text by yourself, trying to reach your own understanding and interpretation. Some students will perhaps be working entirely alone and will be looking for all the help they can get. This short chapter attempts to offer some suggestions of a very basic kind to try to help those who are studying alone, and it may also be of assistance to those on a guided course.

The first question many students ask about working on Chaucer is: 'Should I buy a crib?' The answer is that a 'crib' in the sense of a version that solves all the problems of understanding does not exist and cannot, as we shall see. However, there are several versions of Chaucer rendered into fairly contemporary English, both in prose and verse. An old favourite in rhyme is the 'translation' which has been enjoyed by many generations of students and general readers, by Nevill Coghill. This is inexpensive, and has two other virtues: it is lively reading, and is not cluttered with a mass of notes. If you want to get a rough *impression* of any of *The Canterbury Tales*, you might find this worth considering. It will enable you to read a number of stories quickly and easily, including *The General Prologue*, as introduction and background material to the Miller. Can you, however, use it as a 'translation'?

We said there is no crib to Chaucer. This word is now a little old-fashioned, probably because it was most familiar to those of us of an earlier generation who had to study Latin and Greek. It is possible to get a useful English translation of, say, Livy if you find that historian's Latin too much of a struggle. Latin is a dead language, in the sense that its meaning does not change. Once we have found an acceptable equivalent in English for a Latin word, we can understand what the author means when he uses it. But English is a living language, and changes all the time. At certain periods it has changed very quickly – it was expanding and altering a great deal when Chaucer was writing, and also when Shakespeare was at work. It is changing a lot today – Chambers' *Dictionary of Technical and Scientific English*, which deals only with specialist words, has about 60,000 entries. Shakespeare's vocabulary has been computed at about 15,000 words.

It is, then, not possible to 'translate' Chaucer's shifting tongue into our own shifting tongue, though the attempt can be a challenge and an enjoyment. In the end we have to acquire a feeling for his language, just as, however much French we learn by studying, we shall not feel at home in the language until we have spent a lot of time amongst people who speak nothing else, and begin to pick up a sense of rhythm and idiom and overtone as well as knowing the official uses of the subjunctive.

We can attempt to achieve this familiarity with Chaucer in two ways. The first is by looking systematically at some of the basic difficulties of meaning, the second is by trying to learn something about how his verse actually sounded, when it was originally read aloud to an audience.

Complete beginners may think their greatest difficulty is to understand a single word of what lies before them. Looking for a moment at the opening lines of the tale we have to study, we see this:

> Whylom ther was dwellinge at Oxenford
> A riche gnof, that gestes heeld to bord,
> And of his craft he was a Carpenter.

The words 'whylom' and 'gnof' are utterly unfamiliar, but our notes or glossary may offer us 'formerly' and 'churl' – Skeat's edition does, in fact, give these words. It is not hard for us to recognize old-fashioned spellings of 'there was dwelling at Oxford ... rich ... held guests ... board' and so on, so we cheerfully begin to translate: 'Formerly there was dwelling at Oxford a rich churl who held guests to board, and he was a carpenter of his craft ...' This is an English that never was on land or sea. It makes a kind of sense, but nobody ever has spoken like that or is likely to do. The word 'churl' is not now a spoken word at all, even if we know what it means (someone of low birth). 'Whylom' was a traditional opening, and we still have one – 'Once upon a time'. A man's 'craft' was what we should call his trade or skill. It is soon apparent, as we read on, that the Carpenter is *not* running a lodging house, as our version would suggest, but, having a big house, lets out a room to a student. We do not even say that anyone 'dwells' anywhere now, though we understand the word. There are many editions of Chaucer still in print which give words like 'churl' and so on as if they were current English – and that is exactly what we ought to aim for: Chaucer wrote in the 'modern' English of his day, and if we start translating him using unreal words like 'churl' and 'dwell', and, later on, 'wench' and 'knave', or if we soar off into the pomposities of words like 'scurrility and 'impropriety', as some editions would have us do, we shall never really *feel* Chaucer as what he was – a living author. We have to try to make him sound as though he had just finished writing the story. We shall never succeed – translation is an unending search for what isn't there – but we can do better than our first attempt. So: 'A wealthy fellow once lived at Oxford and took in lodgers. He was a carpenter by trade ...' This is not quite right because 'fellow' does not have the ring of contempt about it that 'gnof' carries – perhaps you would like to think of a better word yourself.

It is fairly easy, in this passage, to spot the obviously difficult words 'gnof' is a striking example of something so strange that we know at once we must look it up What is much more tricky in Chaucer is that many words still exist in the language, but have slightly shifted their meaning. In the very next line we see that he had living with him 'a povre scoler had lerned art' and all these words are with us today – 'a poor scholar (who) had learned art'. This passage is a minefield. Most scholars were poor in those days, so 'poor' is almost a conventional word here; a scholar to us means someone of high academic attainment, but here it seems likely that it means only a student, perhaps an undergraduate; and 'art' in this passage refers to a conventional course of university study, the meaning which survives in Bachelor of Arts, as distinct from the astronomical studies which, we are shortly told, were his real interest – and here we bump our heads on another problem. To Chaucer there was no distinction between astrology and astronomy – they were interrelated, exact sciences, and it is not easy for us in any given context to be sure which to use. Trickier still is the very obvious-looking word that is not to be translated by its modern equivalent – the verb 'can' is a striking example, often meaning 'to be able to' or 'to know how to', a sense which survives in such a question as 'Can you play chess?'

So far we have established that any version we try to make must be in an English which sounds like the language we ourselves actually use, and that we must never take a word for granted, however simple it looks – always check with a good glossary, and, if necessary, update the word given there.

We have now to consider Chaucer's grammar, a word which will probably create a sinking feeling in many readers, as the study of formal grammar has quite gone out of fashion. Take heart. The lengthy tables of forms and endings which appear in many editions are of little practical use to anyone who is not intending to study the whole development of our language from Old English onwards. Grammatical structure was becoming very fluid in Chaucer's own time, and he was almost as free to vary his syntax as he was to spell in his own style. There are certain grammatical signposts which you can learn to spot quite easily, and some of the more important ones are mentioned as they arise in the detailed commentary on the text which follows. A single example of a useful signpost is given here. We nowadays show what grammarians call the past participle by adding '-ed' to the end of a verb – thus to 'call' we make this addition to form 'called', from which past tenses such as 'he has called' may be formed. If you have studied German, you will know that in the same structure something is placed at the *front* of the word – the prefix 'ge-'. Chaucer in this respect shows us the Germanic side of English which he derived directly from what was used before the Norman Conquest. If you see a word which begins with 'y-' such as 'y-clept' you will soon learn to read it as a past participle. This one, a quite common word, in fact means 'called' or 'named'. So, in *The Prologue*, we read of the wives of the self-important Guildsmen, 'It is ful faire to been y-clept "ma dame"' meaning 'It's very nice to be called Madame'. In the tale we are studying a variant spelling appears – 'The which that was y-cleped Absolon' – 'Who was called Absolon' – but the signpost is the same. Most students of Chaucer find it easier by far to absorb these things as they proceed in the study of the text than to sit down and try to learn a mass of tables of grammatical endings – and all the exceptions!

Understanding structure is always easier if we can hear a line spoken, and this leads us to consider how we can learn to 'hear' Chaucer. Most readers are probably aware that pronunciation has changed a great deal since Chaucer's time, and again some editions will present us with long lists of vowels and consonants which are supposed to help us to pronounce Chaucer 'correctly'. They are not very useful to the average learner.

There are two related problems here. You can never enjoy a poem properly unless you can say it or hear someone else do so, since poetry depends on sound as much as, sometimes more than, literal meaning. So we have to try to learn not only how Chaucer pronounced his words, but also how he spoke lines of verse – what is usually called 'scansion'. Chaucer wrote verse in English but used a continental system of scansion for the most part. His poetry is metrical, that is, each line is made up of a number of similar groups or measures (which is all 'metre' means) of sounds. If you try to say aloud 'Pélicans fréquently súffer from bélly-ache' you will find that you are automatically speaking in a regular jingling rhythm. The line breaks up into four little packets of sound, each starting with a heavily stressed syllable followed by two lighter ones. The effect of this 'metre' is mildly comical. Reverse the shape of the measure to two short sounds and a heavier one, as in 'Setting spúrs to my hórse I depárt at great spéed', and you can hear the beat of the hooves. So metres can be used for very different effects. The one which Chaucer used for most of his poetry, and for the tale which we are to study, was to become the most widely used in English, the metre of Shakespeare's plays, of Milton's great poems, the metre which adapts itself most readily to the rhythms of ordinary English speech –

> I wísh I hád a húndred thóusand póunds!

It is easy here to spot the pattern – five groups of sounds, each consisting of a light syllable and a much stronger one. The strong stresses are not all exactly equal or the line would be a mere jingle, but they are there, a quiet undercurrent of music to give shape to the line. In Chaucer's day many words had a light stress at the end, so his version of this metre may have an extra syllable, just as in French.

> The Míller, thát for-drónken wás al pále

shows very clearly the five light stresses, the five heavy ones, and the extra weak sound at the end: the next line lacks the ending and is a straight series of weak–strong sounds –

> So thát unnéthe up-ón his hórs he sát ...

The trick of reading Chaucer, then, is largely a matter of finding the five strong beats, and we cannot do this until we have some idea of how to pronounce the words themselves. A short extract from the early lines of the tale will show us some of the problems:

> With hím there wás dwellínge a póvre scolér,
> Had lérned árt, but ál his fántasýe
> Was túrned fór to lérne astrólogýe,
> And cóude a cérteyn óf conclúsióuns
> To démen bý intérrogációuns,
> Íf that men áxed hím in cértein hóures,
> Whán that men shólde have dróghte or élles shóures ...

The first problem is that not everyone would agree about the placing of some of the stresses – in the last two lines it seems that the first 'measure' of sounds is reversed, with the heavy stress before the light one, but some readers would have it follow the regular pattern; in the first line, in Modern English we should certainly say 'dwélling' and not 'dwellíng', and 'schólar' not 'scholár'. The latter can probably be settled by reference to the rhyme – it rhymes with 'carpenter', which is impossible unless it is the final syllable that is strongly stressed. But most readers will soon be able to pick up the five strong beats which form the basis of the lines while allowing a certain flexibility.

The second problem is to bring us to the matter of pronunciation. In Modern English, 'interrogation' is spoken as five syllables, in-ter-rog-a-tion, the last being sounded 'shun', but in Chaucer it is six – in-ter-rog-ac-i-oun, just as 'conclusion' must have been pronounced as four syllables, con-clu-si-oun. The last 'e' of 'astrologye' and 'fantasye' was pronounced, like the 'houres' and 'shoures' of the final couplet, but Chaucer could drop these final sounds when he wished to – it is clear that 'dwellinge a' was run together, with no separate sound for the 'e', and the same applies to 'lerne astrologye' where the 'e' of 'lerne' is run on into the next vowel. This may seem a troublesome complication, but in practice it means that Chaucer had a great deal of flexibility in his metre – he had many syllables that he could use or drop as suited him. In general, however, we can formulate a rule from this passage – a letter means a sound. This applies not only to vowels, but also to consonants. In the last line quoted, the 'l' of 'sholde' is to be spoken and so is the 'gh' of 'droghte' – the sound is roughly that which a good Scot makes when he speaks of a loch, a rasping aspirate quite unlike the English 'lock' which does duty south of the Border.

This rule – make a letter sound wherever the rhythm allows it – is a good start; but of course no one can learn to pronounce a language from a book, even if he has taken the trouble to master the mysteries of the phonetic alphabet. An hour with a guide who knows how to speak in Chaucerian fashion is worth a volume of instruction. That is why you will be offered no voluminous instructions here. If you have the help of someone with this skill, you need read no further. If you have not, there are two possibilities. Should you have access to a good library with a record-lending department, or to an audio-visual centre with a wide range of tapes and discs, you may be able to listen to recordings of Chaucer made by experts. Of these, one of the earliest was made of the *Prologue* by three scholars – Coghill, Davis and Burrow – which is an excellent introduction to any study of this author (ARGO RG 401). A number of other recordings have since been made, such as the Caedmon (TC 1008) version of parts of *The Pardoner's Tale* and *The Nun's Priest's Tale*; again of special interest is *1000 Years of English Pronunciation* (Lexington LE 7650/55), because it gives not only passages from Chaucer, but ranges from Old English to the eighteenth century, thus enabling us to see – or rather hear – Chaucer in a developing context. *The Miller's Prologue and*

Tale has been recorded for Cambridge Educational by A. C. Spearing, and is available on cassette.

Much here obviously depends upon what resources you may have at your disposal. If you cannot avail yourself of any sort of recording or of a teacher who has this skill, you still have the resource of your own voice. It is not too hard to try to read a little yourself, and can be a lot of fun too. There are three things to bear in mind: the language in which he wrote was a recent amalgam of French and a Germanic tongue, so you will be making French noises for the French-looking words and rather guttural German noises for the shorter, grittier sounds; the spelling may seem offhand at times – it is not even consistent – but it does indicate sounds; and the whole character of the speech was much stronger than that of what we now call Standard English – vowels were fuller, consonants were forcefully pronounced. The last aspect mentioned is very well illustrated in the description of the Miller himself in *The Prologue*. It is worth trying this out, giving full force to *all* the letters, '... short-sholdred, brood, a thikke knarre ... Reed as the bristles of a sowes eres ... A swerd and bokeler bar he ...' The harsh, snarling quality of the sound exactly fits the strong, violent animal-like nature of the man.

A little practice will soon bring confidence – and pleasure. If it brings only modest proficiency, it will also have one other subsidiary benefit. Anyone who has tried to do this will be a little less irritated by the oddities of modern spelling. The letters we now call 'silent' represent sounds that were once made.

4. The Miller and His Language

Chaucer probably never completed the scheme of *The Canterbury Tales*. There are about thirty pilgrims, and each is supposed to tell two stories on the way to the shrine and two on the way back, making a round figure of a hundred and twenty. He wrote twenty-three, some of which are incomplete, and one of which is told by a man who joins the party *en route* – the Canon's Yeoman However, it is clear that he had blocked out some parts of the pattern, including the story with which he intended to conclude – a sermon by the poor Parson – and, luckily for us, the opening group of tales, into which the Miller's contribution comes. From what we have it is also clear that he intended each story to be suitable to the person telling it: the Knight tells a tale of chivalry, the Prioress a legend of a saint, and so on. There are one or two places where this arrangement has been questioned, as in the case of the story told by the Wife of Bath or the tale given to the Merchant, but nowhere is there any obvious lack of compatibility between teller and narrative. In our case, the Miller is very well suited to his subject-matter, and indeed the pattern here is unusually complex, as we are given two pictures of him, not one.

The first, which every serious student of the tale will know, is the portrait of the Miller given in *The General Prologue* to the entire collection. It runs:

> The Miller was a stout carl, for the nones,
> Ful big he was of braun, and eek of bones;
> That proved wel, for over-al ther he cam,
> At wrastling he wolde have alwey the ram.
> He was short-sholdred, brood, a thikke knarre,
> Ther nas no dore that he nolde heve of harre,
> Or breke it, at a renning, with his heed.
> His berd as any sowe or fox was reed,
> And ther-to brood, as though it were a spade.
> Up-on the cop right of his nose he hade
> A werte, and theron stood a tuft of heres,
> Reed as the bristles of a sowes eres;
> His nose-thirles blake were and wyde.
> A swerde and bokeler bar he by his syde;
> His mouth as greet was as a greet forneys.
> He was a janglere and a goliardeys,
> And that was moste of sinne and harlotryes.

Wel coude he stelen corn, and tollen thryes;
And yet he hadde a thombe of gold, pardee.
A whyt cote and a blew hood wered he.
A baggepype wel coude he blowe and sowne,
And ther-with-al he broghte us out of towne.

A rough paraphrase might run as follows – 'The Miller was a sturdy enough rascal with a hefty frame and big muscles. His strength had been well tested because wherever he went he used to win the ram as a prize for wrestling. He was a thick-set, bull-necked fellow, and there was no door that he wouldn't heave off its hinges or split by charging at it head-first. His beard was as red as the hair of a pig or fox, and also broad like a spade. On the bridge of his nose he had a wart on which stood a tuft of hair as red as the bristles in a sow's ears. He had cavernous black nostrils. He carried a sword and round shield at his side. He was a coarse loudmouth and most of his stories were bawdy. He knew very well how to steal corn and take three times his due – and yet, indeed, he had a golden thumb. He wore a white jacket and a blue hood. He could play on and control the wind in the bagpipes very well, and with these he led us out of the town.'

This is full of information, some couched in very carefully chosen terms, and highly relevant to the story he will tell. He is short and thick-set, hairy and very strong; carries weapons; could apparently not only heave a barn-door off its hinges, but split one, perhaps for a drunken wager. The imagery in which he is described is animal – his hair is compared with that of beasts which are cunning and treacherous, his broad, big nostrils suggest an ape, and his mouth – Chaucer says it is as big as the mouth of an oven – utters nothing but coarseness. Millers were notorious thieves, disliked because they enjoyed a monopoly in their own district, and able to swindle because in those times of imprecise measurements it was hard to know just how much flour a given quantity of corn ought to yield. The 'golden thumb' is a reference to a proverb which illustrates this – 'An honest miller has a golden thumb', that is, you won't meet an honest miller in a month of Sundays. The way this is used here seems to mean that he was honest as millers go – not an outrageous thief, but just taking his customary triple profit! The bagpipes were a common peasant instrument, and in medieval art they symbolized lust from the general shape and the tumescence which is produced when they are inflated (blowing is as much an art as playing on this strange instrument, and Chaucer distinguishes the two). The bagpipes acquire added importance later in *The Prologue*, as does the fact that he apparently led the procession.

The full significance of this portrait is not apparent until we have studied the man who always trails alone at the rear of the procession, and also read his story; but some connections are easy to see at once.

Such a tough, pugnacious character will not easily be thwarted, and it is no surprise to us when he insists on being heard as soon as the Knight has finished telling the first story. Though the Host must often have had to deal with drunkards – and the Miller turns out to be very drunk indeed – he cannot shut this one up, and *The Miller's Tale* stands second in the order of the whole. As a man who never stops telling obscene stories, we should expect something in that line from him, and get it; while the general animality of the character suggests that the story will be crude as well as indecent, and certainly there are crude elements in it. Nevertheless, the story is exceedingly well told, and it has been suggested that the most surprising thing about *The Miller's Tale* is that it is a miller who tells it. Chaucer has anticipated this. The Miller is not a fool – he is sly in theft as well as brutal in manner – and men who habitually tell rude stories often learn to tell them well. Today's 'stand-up' comics, especially those who work the working men's clubs of the north, have a repertoire of stories of quite breath-taking indecency – but they deliver it with such skill that the most outraged hearer is often obliged to laugh. Of course, in this tale the artistry is Chaucer's, but he has taken care to tell us enough about the Miller to make the whole thing plausible.

He tells us, in fact, quite a lot more. At the end of the procession rides Oswald the Reeve, a lonely, disagreeable man. He is the opposite of the Miller in every way – old, skinny, hair close-cut, shaven face, silent and apparently shunned by the others. He, like the Miller, carries a sword, but it is rusted in its scabbard. He is also married and was trained to be a carpenter. As soon as the Miller's tale begins, it is evident that it is aimed at the man who rode furthest away from him, the lanky figure of the former carpenter, who is to provide the basis for the duped husband of the story. The Reeve tries to stop this, but the Miller is beyond all intervention. When he has finished, the Reeve immediately insists on telling a story about a Miller, and it is from this that we can gain further insight into the character, since he is very clearly aiming directly at his fellow-pilgrim. Students of the first tale should certainly read the second in full, but here we shall deal briefly with the most important points. The Reeve begins by saying that he will repay the drunken Miller with a story in his own 'cherles termes', and what follows is quite as bawdy as we might expect. The story opens with a description of a miller who is clearly drawn from life – in fact from the Miller himself. Amongst the earliest details in a very full portrait, we are told that he was proud, played the bagpipes, carried a number of weapons and was a feared and dangerous man. He had a broad nose and was a habitual thief. He is also arrogant, and much of his conceit of himself turns on the fact that he has married well – his wife is the (illegitimate) daughter of a priest – though the clergy were unable to marry, these things happened – and his father-in-law has property which he intends to bestow upon the Miller's twenty-year-old daughter, who is consequently kept in very strict confinement until a suitable match appears – we may note that at twenty she is well past the age at which most girls expected to be married, and two years older than the wife of John the Carpenter. The story turns on a number of things: the miller's pride and his thieving; the arrival of two young students to supervise the grinding of their corn; a drunken evening in which the miller becomes well soused; a complicated bedroom farce, in which the miller's daughter and his wife both receive unexpected pleasures; and at the end the miller is left having been soundly thrashed, cuckolded, his daughter's virginity lost and his attempted theft discovered and made good. The parallels with *The Miller's Tale* are obvious – the jealous father replaces the jealous husband, the two young men are in this instance both successful and the one person who is hurt here, the miller himself, is hurt where it is most appropriate – in his family pride and his thieving. Add to this the animal-like nose, the swaggering brutality, the drunkenness and the bagpipes, and we can see how the two men and their two stories complement one another very well indeed.

It is worth noting what Chaucer did next. The Cook – also a big drinker – is so delighted with the Reeve's story that he insists on telling one like it, and launches himself on something which promises to be even more indecent about a young rioter who had a wife that kept a shop for appearance's sake but made her money in bed. At this point appears the cryptic note – 'Chaucer made no more of this story' – which suggests that he well knew when enough was enough. Perhaps he intended to complete it and place it somewhere else in the series. We do not know what he intended to follow it, but in the order in which *The Tales* are usually presented, the next narrator to be called upon is a much more sober character, the Man of Law. Though there are other improper stories, the spate of outright bawdry seems to stop here.

It leaves the modern reader, and more especially the modern translator, with a problem, and one which editors have done little to solve.

The Miller's Language

It was possible for earlier editors of this story to gloss over the impropriety of what happens – adultery, scorched backsides and the like – but they had a real difficulty with the words that are used. Nor is the problem confined to 'Victorian' critics. An edition later than the Swinging Sixties suggests that Chaucer might well apologize for mentioning – obliquely – that pubic hair exists. We believe that few modern readers will feel faint at the sight of what are commonly known as four-letter words, but there may well be a disguised problem here, giving us a false impression of the tone of the tale as Chaucer's contemporaries would have heard it.

The line most editors have taken is that Chaucer excused himself for some of his more outspoken language in *The General Prologue*, as well as in *The Prologue* to this story, on the grounds that to be a truthful artist he had to repeat – he says 'rehearse' – the tales just as they were told, or else falsify his material. The Miller is a 'cherle' and uses coarse expressions, so Chaucer imitates him. If these two supposed apologies are read carefully, we find nothing about such language at all – in *The Miller's Prologue* the apology is for the material, and he says that if we don't want to read this sort of thing we can find other stories whose subject-matter is quite different. In *The General Prologue* he says that he must faithfully record what men say, even though they speak 'rudeliche' – a word which probably means in an uneducated way, not in the elevated, artificial language of courtly romance. He clinches this by saying that Christ himself spoke 'ful brode' in scripture. Jesus, as recorded in the Gospels, used a very plain language, suitable to the simple men to whom he preached. He never uses anything that could be called 'broad language' in the modern sense. The apology is for the general level of speech, not for the use of indecent words, and it seems likely that Chaucer, quite unlike us, had no sense that some words were 'decent' and others were not.

We have no problem of translation – incidentally, anyone reading this book as part of the preparation for an examination in which the candidates are required to give a modern paraphrase of a passage must surely be aware that no examiner would deliberately set an excerpt which contained the sort of language we are talking about – because we can, if we wish, draw upon several different sorts of vocabulary: so we may, if we wish, follow one popular edition and translate 'ers' as 'backside', 'queynte' as 'pudenda' and 'swyve' as 'copulate with'. To many ears at least, the first is acceptably amusing, the other two sound rather more indecent than using the modern derivative of 'queynte', which is 'cunt', while for 'swyve', which has no derivative, the Oxford *Advanced Learner's Dictionary of Current English* offers us 'screw', with a symbol that means we should be careful how we use it in mixed company.

No such dilemma faced Chaucer as the 'taboo' word. The Prioress would not have used some of the words the Miller does simply because she would not have talked about the things he talks about – but if she had had to, she would have used the only vocabulary that was available to her in English.

So did Sir Thomas Malory. Writing about seventy years after Chaucer died, he put together the finest collection of stories of chivalry that the English language contains – *Le Morte D'Arthur*, which has been the inspiration of many writers and the joy of innumerable readers. Glancing into a section with the splendid heading of 'The Noble Tale of Sir Lancelot du Lake', we very shortly find a knight dispatching three others, as follows (in modernized spelling): 'And so straight unto the third knight and smote him behind his horse arse a spear length.' Clearly the writer felt there was no incongruity of language here, and in reading *The Miller's Tale* we should do our best to adopt the same frame of mind. We may not choose to use these words ourselves as a matter of taste or good manners, but should try to remember that such concepts did not attach to language until long after Chaucer's day.

In 1928, D. H. Lawrence published his *Lady Chatterley's Lover*, in which he deliberately used the bluntest of language to try to rid it of the artificial 'improper' associations. His failure is marked by the fact that the book could not be bought in England until, in 1960, it was published in paperback in a deliberate attempt to force a prosecution and establish that one should consider an author's purpose and artistry rather than merely censor his language. The trial was famous – the prosecution failed – and one distinguished writer who gave evidence spoke of Lawrence using words that everybody knows to describe things that everybody does. Chaucer himself urges us not to make too serious a matter out of what was meant for fun. The great French novelist Colette, who read Lawrence's novel in 1932, wrote to a friend in England – 'it's terribly sixth-form and college – what a narrow province obscenity is'. Chaucer would certainly have agreed with the lady, and would be surprised that anyone should think his tale obscene because of the words his characters use.

5. The Text, with Notes

The Knight's Tale, which concerns the idealized love of two cousins for a remote, almost inaccessible, girl, is told with great artistry; but it is over two thousand lines long, and its appeal is chiefly to the intellectual listener with a knowledge of the conventions of courtly love. Though Chaucer has begun his sequence with the teller of highest rank, it would have been rather a trial of the reader's or listener's patience to continue with another of the same kind. The Monk, who is wealthy and worldly and 'fit to be an abbot' as Chaucer says, might seem appropriate in worldly standing to follow the Knight, but it is much more effective to change the level of the story-teller and thus of the story. In fact this tale is also about two young men who are superficially quite similar, both wooing a girl – and one does so in a 'courtly' way, too: the resemblance ends there. The change of social level is neatly accomplished, as we are told in *The Prologue* that the Miller is a drinker, so his noisy interruption of the Host's invitation is natural enough. The Monk, when he finally tells his story, is one of the most boring of them all – he lists some fifteen tragedies in such a laborious way that the Knight finally tells him to stop. Such a dismal catalogue would have been quite out of place at this point in the sequence.

The Miller's Prologue

Whan that the Knight had thus his tale y-told,
In al the route nas ther young ne old
That he ne seyde it was a noble storie,
And worthy for to drawen to memorie;
And namely the gentils everichoon.   5
Our Hoste lough and swoor, 'So moot I goon,
This gooth aright; unbokeled is the male;
Lat see now who shal telle another tale:
For trewely, the game is wel bigonne.
Now telleth ye, sir Monk, if that ye conne,   10
Sumwhat, to quyte with the Knightes tale.'
The Miller, that for-dronken was al pale,
So that unnethe up-on his hors he sat,
He nolde avalen neither hood ne hat,
Ne abyde no man for his curteisye,   15
But in Pilates vois he gan to crye.
And swoor by armes and by blood and bones,
'I can a noble tale for the nones,
With which I wol now quyte the Knightes tale.'
Our Hoste saugh that he was dronke of ale,   20

2–3 *nas . . . ne . . . ne*: Chaucer piles up negatives with a cheerful disregard for the rules: *everyone* agreed it was a fine story.

5 *namely the gentils everichoon*: 'especially every one of the well-born people'. 'Everichoon' is a typical telescoped word, 'every each one'.

6 *Hoste . . . So moot I goon*: the Host of the Tabard Inn, where they had stayed the night before their pilgrimage, who had agreed to go with them and organize the story-telling competition. It is suggested that he may have rigged the draw so that the first story-teller should be the man of highest rank. 'So moot I goon' is one of the many rather meaningless oaths which stud the dialogue – 'As I hope to go on well'.

7 *unbokeled is the male*: 'the bag is unfastened' – that is, the stories have begun.

10 *Now telleth ye*: he addresses the Monk, who appeared in *The Prologue* to be quite rich though his Order prohibited personal possessions, politely as a suitable man of 'rank' in the Church to follow the Knight.

11 *quyte*: 'equal' or 'match', not here in the sense of pay back.

12 *for-*: as a prefix intensifies the word – so he was *very* drunk.

13 *unnethe*: 'scarcely'; as riding was such an everyday activity, a man who could hardly keep his seat had to be thoroughly soused.

14 *He nolde avalen . . . his curteisye*: 'He would take off neither hood nor hat nor give way to anyone out of good manners.' The hood was universal, often with a cap under it: in those days men bared their heads to their superiors generally, not just as a mark of respect for women.

16 *Pilates vois*: Pilate, as performed in the Mystery plays of the period, was loud, ranting villain, and the actor played him with a noisy and melodramatic delivery.

17 *by blood and bones*: this really is blasphemy – he is swearing by the blood and bones of Christ.

18 *'I can a noble tale for the nones'*: 'I know a fine story for this occasion.' 'Can' in Chaucer sometimes has this sense. The expression 'for the nones' is often a mere stop-gap phrase, but here it is meaningful and should be translated.

20 *Our Hoste saugh that he was dronke of ale*: the Host is used to all the stages of drunkenness and thinks he can deal with this troublesome and potentially dangerous man – the Miller was very strong and a good fighter – by soothing words. When a heavy drinker has had so much that he is 'al pale' (l. 12) he is commonly beyond thinking one thought at a time. The Miller knows only that someone has been speaking and now he wishes to have his turn.

And seyde: 'Abyd, Robin, my leve brother,
Som bettre man shall telle us first another:
Abyd, and lat us werken thriftily.'
'By goddes soul,' quod he, 'that wol nat I;
For I wol speke, or elles go my wey.'   25
Our Hoste answerde: 'Tel on, a devel wey!
Thou art a fool, thy wit is overcome.'
'Now herkneth,' quod the Miller, 'alle and some!
But first I make a protestacioun
That I am dronke, I knowe it by my soun;   30
And therfore, if that I misspeke or seye,
Wyte it the ale of Southwerk, I yow preye;
For I wol telle a legende and a lyf
Bothe of a Carpenter, and of his wyf,
How that a clerk hath set the wrightes cappe.'   35

The story is given greater impact by being directed at one of the other
pilgrims. The Reeve is described in *The Prologue* as lean and mean-looking
in every way, and disliked and feared by all the tenant farmers whose
returns to their feudal lord it was his job to collect and check. He is also
elderly and taciturn, riding always at the rear of the procession, as far
from the Miller as he can get. We are told that he was taught a useful trade
in his youth – he was a carpenter. His age and unpopularity make him
a likely butt for the Miller's robust humour – though he has his revenge
by telling a story of equal vigour about a rascally Miller whose womenfolk
are the object of the amorous attentions of two young men.

The Reve answerde and seyde, 'Stint thy clappe,
Lat be thy lewed dronken harlotrye.
It is a sinne and eek a greet folye
To apeiren any man, or him diffame,
And eek to bringen wyves in swich fame.   40
Thou mayst y-nogh of othere thinges seyn.'
This dronken Miller spak ful sone ageyn,
And seyde, 'Leve brother Osewold,
Who hath no wyf, he is no cokewold.

21 *Abyd, Robin, my leve brother*: 'Steady on, my dear brother Robin, wait a bit.'

22 *bettre*: the word is not insulting – he means someone of higher rank.

23 *thriftily*: not quite in the modern sense: 'in the most profitable way' comes close.

26 *Tel on, a devel wey!*: 'Carry on and be damned to you!' The Host quickly realizes what sort of a drunk he is dealing with, and cuts his losses.

29 *protestacioun*: a ponderous word. Drunks often seem fascinated by the difficulty they have in pronouncing long words, and do so with great care and gravity – hence all those jokes about being under the affluence of incohol. We can almost hear the man getting his tongue round this word, which had five syllables then.

31 *if that I misspeke or seye*: 'if I say what I shouldn't, or mispronounce anything'.

32 *Wyte it the ale of Southwerk*: 'Blame it on the beer from Southwark' – an unkind jeer at the Host, whose inn was there and whose drink the Miller had been tanking up with before they set out. He implies that on *good* beer he is in command of his tongue.

35 *How that a clerk hath set the wrightes cappe*: this line has several problem words in it. A clerk could be a clergyman, a student, a graduate, simply someone who was literate: in the Oxford context of the story which follows, 'student' seems most apt. A 'wright' was any kind of workman – it comes from the old irregular form of the verb 'to work' which partly survives in 'wrought iron' – and to set someone's 'cappe' was to make a fool of him.

36 *The Reve answerde ...*: the Reeve picks up the allusion instantly. He was trained as a carpenter and he and the Miller dislike each other.

37 *lewed*: the word had then the sense of 'ignorant' rather than 'crude' or 'vulgar'; harlotry was literally talking about harlots (as pornography is writing about them), so rude stories generally.

39 *To apeiren any man, or him diffame*: 'to injure or slander any man'.

40 *bringen wyves in swich fame*: 'fame' here means 'notoriety' – 'make women infamous'.

41 *Thou mayst y-nogh of othere thinges seyn*: 'There are plenty of other things you can talk about.'

44 *cokewold*: 'cuckold' is a convenient word for a husband whose wife deceives him (it is connected, for obvious reasons, with the cuckoo and the idea that it takes a clever man to be sure who is father to his child) but it is now rather literary and there is no substitute. 'Deceived husband' is accurate but pompous.

But I sey nat therfore that thou art oon;   45
Ther been ful gode wyves many oon,
And ever a thousand gode ayeyns oon badde,
That knowestow wel thy-self, but-if thou madde.
Why artow angry with my tale now?
I have a wyf, pardee, as wel as thou,   50
Yet nolde I, for the oxen in my plogh,
Taken up-on me more than y-nogh,
As demen of my-self that I were oon;
I wol beleve wel that I am noon.
An housbond shal nat been inquisitif   55
Of goddes privetee, nor of his wyf.
So he may finde goddes foyson there,
Of the remenant nedeth nat enquere.'

   Before beginning the story, Chaucer offers an apology – or, more
correctly, a warning comment – about its content. As has been earlier
suggested, this is less to do with the language in which the tale is told than
with its material. He repeats what he says in *The Prologue*, that it is his
duty to repeat stories as truthfully as he can, and this story is certainly
true to its teller. His advice to the prudish reader – if you don't like it,
choose another – is as sound today as when it was written; there are still
plenty of people who seem more ready to telephone angrily to the broad-
casters of material they do not like than simply to switch off or seek
another programme.

What sholde I more seyn, but this Millere
He nolde his wordes for no man forbere,   60
But tolde his cherles tale in his manere;
Me thinketh that I shal reherce it here.
And ther-fore every gentil wight I preye,
For goddes love, demeth nat that I seye
Of evel entente, but that I moot reherce   65
Hir tales alle, be they bettre or werse,
Or elles falsen som of my matere.
And therfore, who-so list it nat y-here,
Turne over the leef, and chese another tale;
For he shal finde y-nowe, grete and smale,   70

47-8 *And ever a thousand ... but-if thou madde*: 'And there are always a thousand good married women for every bad one, as you must know yourself unless you are crazy.' The Miller is sarcastic in his heavy-handed way. Medieval thought held that women were by nature wanton, starting with Eve flirting with the seductive serpent.

51-3 *Yet nolde I ... that I am noon*: 'Yet I would not be prepared to assume too readily that I am a cuckold – not for the oxen in my plough.' This is rather an ambiguous remark: he appears to accept the innate unreliability of married women but would not make bets either way on his own marriage. Ploughs were then drawn by oxen, not horses, and were so in some areas until the present century.

55-6 *An housbond ... of his wyf*: 'A husband should not be too curious about his wife's private affairs or God's.' This introduces a notion which is to be important in the story – the secret purposes of God – and a rude pun on 'privetee', which could then mean what we still sometimes call 'private parts'.

57 *foyson*: 'plenty'. The sentiment is vigorously advocated by the Wife of Bath, who says that if a man gets good light from a lantern, he should not begrudge it if someone lights a candle from it for himself. The lantern continues to give undiminished light to its owner.

60 *He nolde his wordes for no man forbere*: 'He would not restrain his speech for anyone.' As a 'cherl', a man of low breeding, he tells a rude story. Chaucer turns aside from the narration to address his readers, explaining (ll. 63–7), as he has already done in *The General Prologue*, that it is his duty to 'reherce' each story faithfully, and this is not done with 'evel entente' but in order not to 'falsify his material'.

68 *who-so list if nat y-here*: 'y-here' is the typical way of making a past participle. The grammatical pattern is 'whoever does not want it heard'.

69 *leef*: the reference to the 'leaf' shows us how casual Chaucer can be – he has slipped from the supposed narrator to the author of a book, and his audience have become readers.

70 *grete and smale*: ambiguous – it may refer to the stories, which vary in length and seriousness, or to the readers of whatever rank.

Of storial thing that toucheth gentillesse,
And eek moralitee and holinesse;
Blameth nat me if that ye chese amis.
The Miller is a cherl, ye know wel this;
So was the Reve, and othere many mo,   75
And harlotrye they tolden bothe two.
Avyseth yow and putte me out of blame;
And eek men shal nat make ernest of game.   78

Here endeth the prologe.

Here biginneth the Millere his tale.

Whylom ther was dwellinge at Oxenford
A riche gnof, that gestes heeld to bord,   80
And of his craft he was a Carpenter.
With him ther was dwellinge a povre scoler,
Had lerned art, but al his fantasye
Was turned for to lerne astrologye,
And coude a certeyn of conclusiouns   85
To demen by interrogaciouns,
If that men axed him in certein houres,
Whan that men sholde have droghte or elles shoures,
Or if men axed him what sholde bifalle
Of every thing, I may nat rekene hem alle.   90

Chaucer begins by introducing his 'hero', so far as the story may be said to have one. Each character is presented in a different way, and that chosen for Nicholas is unusual – he is described almost entirely through his room and his possessions. His own appearance is not mentioned – only his manner, and that he smelled pleasantly.

71–2 *gentillesse ... moralitee ... holinesse*: 'gentillesse' is notoriously hard to put into modern English, though it is a central concept to *The Knight's Tale*, for instance. It is everything that we tend to think of under the heading of chivalrous conduct – strength's obligation to the weak, greatness to lowliness, humility, courage, devotion to your cause, your lady, your faith. 'Moralitee' here means rather moral discussion as compared with the third term, 'holinesse', which refers more to behaviour, to simple saintliness. So the Knight and Franklyn tell stories of the first quality, the Clerk raises a moral issue to do with obedience in marriage and the Prioress tells a legend of a boy saint who lived and died in holiness.

76 *So was the Reve*: the Reeve's story is as scandalous as the Miller's.

78 *eek men shal nat make ernest of game*: a fair reminder – this is frivolous, don't take it too seriously.

79 *Whylom ... Oxenford*: 'whylom' – 'once upon a time', a stock opening. The setting of Oxford, whose old spelling survives in the 'Oxon' which its graduates use after their degree, is to be balanced by the Cambridge setting for the Reeve's story.

80 *A riche gnof, that gestes heeld to bord*: 'gnof' originally meant a thief – here a rather contemptuous term, perhaps 'fellow' used sneeringly. That he took in lodgers, or at least one lodger, is no special sign of meanness or poverty. Life was much less private in those days, and if he had a big house it was sensible to let some of it.

83–4 *al his fantasye ... astrologye*: 'his whole desire was to study astrology'. 'Astrologye' was not then thought of as distinct from astronomy, but was a science. The passage which follows uses some of its vocabulary – Chaucer himself seems to have been a keen astronomer/astrologer.

85–90 *And coude a certeyn ... hem alle*: the general sense is that he knew how to carry out some procedures to answer questions about what times were likely to bring rain or drought – a constant worry to farmers. He was also consulted on other matters to do with the future.

This clerk was cleped hende Nicholas;
Of derne love he coude and of solas;
And ther-to he was sleigh and ful privee,
And lyk a mayden meke for to see.
A chambre hadde he in that hostelrye   95
Allone, with-outen any companye,
Ful fetisly y-dight with herbes swote;
And he him-self as swete as is the rote
Of licorys, or any cetewale.
His Almageste and bokes grete and smale,   100
His astrelabie, longinge for his art,
His augrim-stones layen faire a-part
On shelves couched at his beddes heed:
His presse y-covered with a falding reed.
And al above ther lay a gay sautrye,   105
On which he made a nightes melodye
So swetely, that all the chambre rong;
And *Angelus ad virginem* he song;
And after that he song the kinges note;
Ful often blessed was his mery throte.   110
And thus this swete clerk his tyme spente
After his freendes finding and his rente.

91   *This clerk was cleped hende Nicholas*: two problem words here are 'clerk' and 'hende'. The first is again most easily rendered as 'student' in the Oxford context; 'hende', which means vaguely 'polite' or 'fine', is attached to his name throughout, and is either a heavy sarcasm or so conventional that it does not need to be translated – a sort of nickname, almost.

92   *Of derne love he coude and of solas*: 'He knew all about secret love-affairs and their satisfaction.'

96   *Allone*: it is a distinct mark of his character that he has a room to himself: privacy was a scarce commodity then, and most people expected to share rooms and often beds in, for example, inns and lodgings.

97   *Ful fetisly y-dight with herbes swote*: 'pleasantly decorated with fragrant plants'. In a rather smelly age this is a fastidious touch, as is the way in which he keeps himself as fresh as liquorice-root or ginger (l. 99).

100–105   *His Almageste ... a gay sautrye*: if he owned a copy of the Almagest (literally 'Great Work') by the famous Alexandrian astronomer Ptolemy, and other books, all hand-written and very expensive, he must have done well out of his consultations. An astrolabe (l. 101), a sort of sextant for taking the height of stars, on whose use Chaucer wrote an instruction-book for his son, could be quite costly, too. Augrim-stones (l. 102) were a form of portable abacus used on a checked cloth or board to do arithmetical calculations. We note that all his possessions had their proper place. Even his cupboard (l. 104) is covered by a red woven cloth, on top of which he has a handsome psaltery, or small harp (l. 105).

108–9   *Angelus ad virginem ... kinges note*: *Angelus ad Virginem* was a hymn about the Annunciation, and there may be a blasphemous overtone here – Nicholas's intentions when he approaches Alison are rather more down-to-earth than those in the hymn, and she is scarcely virginal. The 'kinges note' may be a popular song of the time.

112   *rente*: simply 'income'.

The marital situation is now briefly but clearly presented. The old Carpenter has married a much younger girl – though at eighteen she is quite old for marriage by medieval standards – and the implication seems clear that he was able to afford her, rather as a luxury. Having secured himself someone so attractive, he makes matters worse for the girl by being extremely possessive. It is hardly a compensation to dress her so expensively. The situation was a familiar one in comedy and still is – the middle-aged mogul acquiring an over-lively consort and buying her mink and diamonds ...

This Carpenter had wedded newe a wyf
Which that he lovede more than his lyf;
Of eightetene yeer she was of age.   115
Jalous he was, and heeld hir narwe in cage,
For she was wilde and yong, and he was old,
And demed him-self ben lyk a cokewold.
He knew nat Catoun, for his wit was rude,
That bad man sholde wedde his similitude.   120
Men sholde wedden after hir estaat,
For youthe and elde is often at debaat.
But sith that he was fallen in the snare,
His moste endure, as other folk, his care.

113   *newe*: 'recently'.

115   *Of eightetene yeer she was of age*: eighteen was quite old to be getting married – but old enough to be hungry for more than perhaps her aged husband could provide.

116   *heeld her narwe in cage*: 'kept her caged up' – an important line, because it suggests that what follows is partly his own fault. More liberality and less suspicion and restriction might have prevented her adultery. Indeed, in l. 118, he seems almost to bring upon himself what he feared.

119   *He knew nat Catoun, for his wit was rude*: he did not know the Latin collection of moralizing verses of Dionysius Cato, because his mind was uneducated.

121   *estaat*: 'condition', often of rank, here of age.

122   *youthe and elde is often at debaat*: 'youth and age are often in conflict'. This sounds like a proverb and may be meant as a contrast with the book-learnt wisdom of Cato.

123–4   *But sith that ... his care*: this reinforces the idea of 'Serve him right'. If he insisted on entering into this dangerous alliance, he must put up with the consequences.

There follows one of Chaucer's fullest and most famous portraits. While admiring the skill of the passage – Alison is largely described through her dress, but we learn much physical detail, even how she tasted – we should not be blind to the warmth of the account. No doubt Chaucer, like most men, did not find it hard to look at a sexy young lady. He has brought her fully to life here, not only to give vitality and credibility to the story, but also to make us so aware of the girl's attraction that we shall not sit in judgement on her for her subsequent conduct.

Fair was this yonge wyfe, and ther-with-al	125
As any wesele hir body gent and smal.	
A ceynt she werede barred al of silk,	
A barmclooth eek as whyt as the morne milk	
Up on hir lendes, ful of many a gore.	
Whyt was hir smok and brouded al bifore	130
And eek bihinde, on hir coler aboute,	
Of col-blak silk, with-inne and eek with-oute.	
The tapes of hir whyte voluper	
Were of the same suyte of hir coler;	
Hir filet brood of silk, and set ful hye:	135
And sikerly she hadde a likerous yë.	
Ful smale y-pulled were hir browes two,	
And tho were bent, and blake as any sloo.	

125 *Fair*: this then meant simply 'good-looking', not necessarily 'blonde'.

126 *As any wesele hir body gent and smal*: 'Her body was as sleek and slender as a weasel.' 'Smal' is a trap – it normally means slim. Weasels, like ferrets, which mate for hours and can, it is said, die of frustration, are sexy creatures.

127–9 *A ceynt ... many a gore*: the slender waist is emphasized by a belt ('ceynt') of expensive striped silk. Her apron ('barmcloth') is as white as fresh milk, before the cream has risen to tinge it yellow, and, with its many pleats swinging about her thighs ('lendes'), emphasizes both waist and hips.

130–32 *Whyt was hir smok ... and eek with-oute*: 'smok' is a difficulty. It came to mean a loose undergarment, a shift, but in medieval times it could also mean an outer garment, like the 'smock frock' of nineteenth-century labourers, gathered up in elaborate pleats still known as smocking. Since we are told so much about it, it seems that it is her dress rather than what is worn underneath it. This is embroidered, back and front, with silk as black as charcoal (the 'col' of the time was not likely to be mineral) and the same embroidery was continued on the inside as well as the outside of her collar.

This elaborate dress, so carefully described, serves several purposes. The picture itself is charming – a slim young girl with her waist tightly belted and a full-pleated apron swinging round her hips below it; the colour-scheme is bold and fresh – black and white; and the costume implies that she did no work (we later find they had a couple of servants) and that her husband was prepared to spend money on her, since such a get-up would be expensive. He is no doubt trying to keep her faithful by spoiling her.

133 *voluper*: a head-covering, tied under the chin with tapes.

134 *of the same suyte of*: 'matched'.

135 *Hir filet brood of silk, and set ful hye*: 'She had a broad head-band of silk, pushed well up' – to show off her high forehead, then such an esteemed mark of female beauty that ladies who did not have one used to shave part of the hair away at the front to achieve an egg-like oval.

136 *And sikerly she hadde a likerous yë*: 'and she certainly had a sexy eye'.

137 *Ful smale y-pulled were hir browes two*: 'Her eyebrows were plucked slenderly.' At that period any form of cosmetic treatment was regarded as wanton, except in the very great. In the next line we learn that she plucked them into arcs (bent) and that they were as black as a sloe, the fruit of the blackthorn.

She was ful more blisful on to see
Than is the newe pere-jonette tree;   140
And softer than the wolle is of a wether
And by hir girdel heeng a purs of lether
Tasseld with silk, and perled with latoun.
In al this world, to seken up and doun,
Ther nis no man so wys, that coude thenche   145
So gay a popelote, or swich a wenche.
Ful brighter was the shyning of hir hewe
Than in the tour the noble y-forged newe.
But of hir song, it was as loude and yerne
As any swalwe sittinge on a berne.   150
Ther-to she coude skippe and make game,
As any kide or calf folwinge his dame.
Hir mouth was swete as bragot or the meeth,
Or hord of apples leyd in hey or heeth.
Winsinge she was, as is a joly colt,   155
Long as a mast, and upright as a bolt.
A brooch she baar up-on hir lowe coler,
As brood as is the bos of a bocler.
Hir shoes were laced on hir legges hye;
She was a prymerole, a pigges-nye   160
For any lord to leggen in his bedde,
Or yet for any good yeman to wedde.

The plot now opens with Nicholas's bid for the girl. His technique of seduction is interesting in two ways. He combines a highly physical approach, designed to make the girl aware of his young, urgent body, with the verbal protestations of the conventional courtly lover – that he will die if he does not have her love and so on; and this is in sharp contrast with the ineffectual tactics adopted by his rival. It has been suggested that the scene might have an extra edge for the medieval hearers, in that it is a sort of parody of the Annunciation. If so, Chaucer was playing with blasphemy to a dangerous extent.

140 *pere-jonette*: this may have been chosen for two reasons: the fruit is sweet and the tree bears and ripens early. Alison is precocious, which means literally 'pre-cooked', and delicious.

141 *wether*: 'sheep'. The term is now only used in 'bell-wether', a sheep which acts as a sort of leader to a flock at pasture.

143 *perled with latoun*: her purse was studded with an alloy rather like brass, which was often used as a cheap substitute for gold: among the pilgrims, the Pardoner has a cross made of this metal.

144–6 *In al this world ... swich a wenche*: 'No man is clever enough, if he searched the whole world, to fancy such a dishy poppet or such a piece.' The original is very colloquial and not very polite – 'wench' implied something more than just a girl.

147–8 *Ful brighter ... y-forged newe*: 'She was brighter than a newly minted noble from the Tower.' A noble was a coin, and the Royal Mint was originally in the Tower of London.

149 *yerne*: 'lively'. The comparison with a swallow (l. 150), not noted for its song, is odd – but it is a beautiful and graceful bird in flight.

151 *Ther-to she coude skippe and make game*: 'And also she could prance about and play.'

153–4 *Her mouth ... in hey or heeth*: 'Her mouth was as fresh as drinks made from honey, or apples stored in hay or heather.' In those days of poor dental hygiene, a fresh mouth was a very real asset: bragot is a mixture of beer and honey, mead is fermented honey and both are delicious and insidiously intoxicating; good apples stored in sweet hay are very fragrant. The whole passage is sensous, though in an inoffensive way.

155–6 *Winsinge she was ... as a bolt*: 'She was as frisky as a fine young horse, tall and straight as an arrow.' A 'bolt' was usually the term for a crossbow-arrow, which was accurately made to slide in its groove.

157–8 *A brooch she baar ... of a bocler*: the brooch – as big as the boss in the middle of a round shield – is strategically placed at the apex of her low-cut collar to draw attention to what lies below.

159 *Hir shoes were laced on hir legges high*: in praising her neatly fastened boots, the author implies that she let us see more of her legs than was then considered proper.

160 *She was a prymerole, a pigges-nye*: 'She was a primrose, a sweetie-pie.'

161–2 *For any lord ... yeman to wedde*: a lord could take a mistress, a middle-class man married.

Now sire, and eft sire, so bifel the cas,
That on a day this hende Nicholas
Fil with this yonge wyf to rage and pleye,   165
Whyl that hir housbond was at Oseneye,
As clerkes ben ful subtile and ful queynte;
And prively he caughte hir by the queynte;
And seyde, 'Y-wis, but if ich have my wille,
For derne love of thee, lemman, I spille.'   170
And heeld hir harde by the haunche-bones,
And seyde, 'Lemman, love me al at-ones,
Or I wol dyen, also god me save!'
And she sprong as a colt doth in the trave,
And with hir heed she wryed faste awey,   175
And seyde, 'I wol nat kisse thee, by my fey,
Why, lat be,' quod she, 'lat be, Nicholas,
Or I wol crye out "harrow" and "allas".
Do wey your handes for your curteisye!'
This Nicholas gan mercy for to crye,   180
And spak so faire, and profred hir so faste,
That she hir love him graunted atte laste,
And swoor hir ooth, by seint Thomas of Kent,
That she wol been at his comandement,
When that she may hir leyser wel espye.   185
'Myn housbond is so ful of jalousye,
That but ye wayte wel and been privee,
I woot right wel I nam but deed,' quod she.
'Ye moste been ful derne, as in this cas.'
'Nay ther-of care thee noght,' quod Nicholas,   190
'A clerk had litherly biset his whyle,
But-if he coude a carpenter bigyle.'
And thus they been acorded and y-sworn
To wayte a time, as I have told biforn.

163 *Now sire ... so bifel the cas*: 'Now, gentlemen, it so happened that ...'

165 *rage and pleye*: 'fool about' (but with a serious purpose).

166 *Oseneye*: Osney, now lost in the suburbs of Oxford, had an Augustinian abbey.

168 *And prively he caughte hir by the queynte*: 'And secretly he grabbed hold of her by –' and here the reader must take his choice of modern words: the sudden, saucy attack upon her person can leave her in no doubt of his intentions.

170 *For derne love of thee, lemman, I spille*: a part-parody of the language of refined, courtly love. It means 'I am dying for love of you, darling,' but has suggestive undertones: a 'lemman' was a rather crude word for a sweetheart, and 'spille' may imply something more sexual than death.

174 *she sprong as a colt doth in the trave*: 'She started like a young horse in the shoeing-frame.' The trave, a sort of tent-shaped framework, to each leg of which one of the beast's fetlocks is lashed, is still used in Wyoming and makes the wildest creature very helpless indeed. Her responses (ll. 176–9) – 'take away your hands' – 'I'll shout for help' – 'be kind enough to take your hands off me' – do not seem very earnest, and she does *not* raise the traditional cry for help of the time, 'harrow!'

180 *gan mercy for to crye*: 'begged her to show him pity'. This is 'courtly' speech.

181 *profred hir so faste*: 'urged her so much'. But some texts read 'profred *him* so faste', which would mean 'urged *himself* upon her so vigorously', and seems in general line with his assault tactics. She would thus be aware of his excited young body, and perhaps compare it with the less urgent approaches of her husband.

183 *seint Thomas of Kent*: Thomas à Becket, to whose shrine – the most famous in England, and of international repute too – the pilgrims are riding.

188 *I nam but deed*: 'I am as good as dead'. 'Nam' is a typical contraction of the time – 'I ne am' in full, so 'I'm nothing but dead', literally.

191–2 *A clerk ... carpenter bigyle*: 'A student has been wasting his time if he can't make a fool of a carpenter.'

193–4 *And thus they been ... wayte a time*: 'So they have agreed and promised to wait for a suitable time.'

Whan Nicholas had doon thus everydeel,   195
And thakked hir about the lendes weel,
He kist hir swete, and taketh his sautrye,
And pleyeth faste, and maketh melodye.
Than fil it thus, that to the parish-chirche,
Cristes owne werkes for to wirche,   200
This gode wyf went on an haliday;
Hir forheed shoon as bright as any day,
So was it wasshen whan she leet hir werk.

The second contender for Alison's favours is now introduced – and again character is presented by a different means: Absolon is largely described by his appearance, with special emphasis on his hair, a symbol of vanity and of his narcissistic nature, emphasized by his dress.

Now was ther of that chirche a parish-clerk,
The which that was y-cleped Absolon.   205
Crul was his heer, and as the gold it shoon,
And strouted as a fanne large and brode;
Ful streight and even lay his joly shode.
His rode was reed, his eyen greye as goos;
With Powles window corven on his shoos,   210

195–7 *Whan Nicholas ... his sautrye*: 'So, when Nicholas had done all this and felt her up well round the thighs, he kissed her delightfully and took his harp.' Again there is the mixture of the very physical tactic and something more subtle – here, the use of music: presumably the kisses were 'swete' to Alison. It is not now hard to see why she was so easily won: Nicholas is young, vigorous, accomplished and quite clear about what he wants. The contrast with her lawful spouse is implicit.

200 *Cristes owne werkes for to wirche*: 'to do the things Christ ordered', that is to attend service and pray.

201 *gode*: presumably ironic. A haliday was a holy day – our holiday – and there were well over a hundred saints' days in the medieval calendar when attendance at Mass was expected of the devout.

202 *Hir forheed shoon as bright as any day*: the famous forehead again! She has washed it specially when she had finished her work.

204 *parish-clerk*: a parish clerk had various duties in the church, and might be in what were called Minor Orders: that is, he was not a priest, but could, for example, carry the thurible in which incense was burned.

205 *Absolon*: the biblical story of Absalom, son of David, who rebelled against his father and was captured because of his long hair, which got tangled up in a thicket when he was trying to escape, was a familiar subject of medieval homilies on human vanity.

206 *Crul*: an example of metathesis, the reversing of a vowel and a consonant, especially an 'r' – the modern form is 'curled'.

207 *And strouted as a fanne large and brode*: 'and spread out wide like a fan'. The fan is a winnowing fan used in throwing roughly threshed grain into the air and wafting away the husks; a large, shell-shaped object.

208 *his joly shode*: 'his handsome parting'. Absolon's preoccupation with his hair is an early signal of his personal vanity and downfall.

209 *His rode was reed, his eyen greye as goos*: 'he had a ruddy complexion'. Grey eyes were fashionable.

210 *With Powles window corven on his shoos*: his shoes had ornamental patterns cut into them, like the famous window of (old) Saint Paul's, which was destroyed in the Fire of London. It was the largest rose window in England, one of the largest in Europe.

In hoses rede he wente fetisly.
Y-clad he was ful smal and proprely,
Al in a kirtel of a light wachet;
Ful faire and thikke been the poyntes set.
And ther-up-on he hadde a gay surplys   215
As whyte as is the blosme up-on the rys.
A mery child he was, so god me save,
Wel coude he laten blood and clippe and shave,
And make a chartre of lond or acquitaunce.
In twenty manere coude he trippe and daunce   220
After the scole of Oxenforde tho,
And with his legges casten to and fro,
And pleyen songes on a small rubible;
Ther-to he song som-tyme a loud quinible;
And as wel coude he pleye on his giterne.   225
In al the toun nas brewhous ne taverne
That he ne visited with his solas,
Ther any gaylard tappestere was.
But sooth to seyn, he was somdel squaymous
Of farting, and of speche daungerous.   230
This Absolon, that jolif was and gay,
Gooth with a sencer on the haliday,
Sensinge the wyves of the parish faste;
And many a lovely look on hem he caste,
And namely on this carpenteres wyf.   235
To loke on hir him thoughte a mery lyf,
She was so propre and swete and likerous.
I dar wel seyn, if she had been a mous,
And he a cat, he wolde hir hente anon.

212   *smal*: his clothes were slim-fitting to emphasize his figure.

213–16   *Al in a kirtel ... up-on the rys*: 'In a light-blue jacket ... over which he wore a surplice (when officiating in church) as white as the blossom on the bough.' The 'poyntes' were the ends of the laces with which the jacket was fastened, and these were often decorative metal tags.

218–19   *Wel coude he laten blood ... lond or acquitaunce*: 'He was skilful in blood-letting and shaving and could draw up conveyances of property or deeds of settlement.' The first two skills went together, barber-surgeons being licensed to perform minor operations such as blood-letting (as the bloodstained bandage round the barber's pole still suggests). Lawyers were expensive, and his ability to draw up documents must have been useful.

221   *After the scole of Oxenforde*: 'in the style which was then fashionable at Oxford'.

223   *And pleyen songes on a small rubible*: 'and play tunes on a small fiddle'.

224   *quinible*: perhaps best translated as 'falsetto', as it is an artificially high voice, somewhat like a counter-tenor. The suggestion of effeminacy is quite wrong – the voice is artificially acquired – but Chaucer seems to lean on this popular view of it.

228   *Ther any gaylard tappestere was*: 'where there was a lively barmaid' (or woman innkeeper). He liked to show off to pretty women, apparently.

229–30   *he was somdel squaymous ... of speche daungerous*: 'he was a bit squeamish about such bodily functions as breaking wind, and fastidious in speech'. Medieval people were generally not so fussy – and this nicety on his part is important later on.

232   *sencer*: 'incense-burner', or 'thurible'.

234   *lovely*: 'loving', 'amorous'.

237   *She was so propre and swete and likerous*: 'She was so perfectly delicious – and sexy.'

We are now shown **Absolon's** approach to the problem of winning a lady: it begins with a conventional approach – a serenade. His unrealistic attitude is ridiculed – he sings his song when her husband is with her, and his voice – well-known through the town, as we have already been told – is immediately recognized. This is not a very auspicious beginning.

This parish-clerk, this joly Absolon,   240
Hath in his herte swich a love-longinge,
That of no wyf ne took he noon offringe;
For curteisye, he seyde, he wolde noon.
The mone, whan it was night, ful brighte shoon,
And Absolon his giterne hath y-take,   245
For paramours, he thoghte for to wake.
And forth he gooth, jolif and amorous,
Til he cam to the carpenteres hous
A litel after cokkes hadde y-crowe;
And dressed him up by a shot-windowe   250
That was up-on the carpenteres wal.
He singeth in his vois gentil and smal,
'Now, dere lady, if thy wille be,
I preye yow that ye wol rewe on me,'
Ful wel acordaunt to his giterninge.   255
This carpenter awook, and herd him singe,
And spak un-to his wyf, and seyde anon,
'What! Alison! herestow nat Absolon
That chaunteth thus under our boures wal?'
And she answerde hir housbond ther-with-al,   260
'Yis, god wot, John, I here it every-del.'
This passeth forth; what wol ye bet than wel?

240   *joly*: Absolon is called 'joly' much as Nicholas is called 'hende', and perhaps with as little meaning – but one sense was 'pretty', which goes with the suggestion of a certain effeminacy.

242–3   *That of no wyf . . . he wolde noon*: 'Out of good manners, he said, he would not accept an offering from any woman.' A 'wyf' was any adult woman. The offerings, of course, were to the Church, not him.

245   *giterne*: to go serenading he does not take his fiddle but the more conventional instrument for the job, an early sort of guitar.

249–50   *A litel after . . . shot-windowe*: time was not a very precise matter then – cocks start to crow some time before dawn. The window that he leans himself up against is an important part of the story, so we are told that it is a 'shot' window, that is one made to open and shut. It appears later that it is hinged at the top.

252   *gentil and smal*: 'refined and light'. The high-pitched style of his singing reduces volume, so the word for 'slender' is apt.

253–4   *Now, dere lady . . . rewe on me*: 'If it is your desire, dear lady, I beg you to have pity on me.' This formal, courtly plea is well accompanied on his guitar. The whole situation is absurd. Few girls want to be woken in the small hours by empty compliments of this sort – and her husband is with her . . .

257–9   *and seyde anon . . . our boures wal?*: 'and he immediately said, "Hey! Alison! don't you hear Absolon singing like that under our bedroom wall?" ' (The form 'herestow' is a typical running-together of 'hearest-thou'.) The Carpenter would recognize the voice at once for two reasons: the singer was well-known for his voice around the town, and Oxford was then, like most towns, very small, so everyone knew everyone else. Absolon can hardly have supposed his serenading would have passed unheard and unrecognized. A 'boure' was a rather fancy word for a bedroom, derived from the 'ladies' bower' of great houses.

261   *Yis, got wot, John, I here it every-del*: Alison's reply does not suggest that she favours this approach. The colloquial 'Yis' with which she begins serves to sound a note of downright irritation – 'Yes, God knows, John, I hear every single note!' She does not care to be disturbed by such a silly wooing. In this line, incidentally, we learn the Carpenter's name. It is perhaps of some slight point that Chaucer gives him the commonest name – allowing for local forms – in all Europe. We have already seen that Absolon's name had a special relevance. Nicholas comes from the Greek *nike*, victory.

262   *This passeth forth; what wol ye bet than wel?*: 'So things went on. What more do you want?'

Absolon continues his wooing in a sort of travesty of the way in which courtly love was conducted: this involved the use of intermediaries, and the offering of gifts, as well as demonstrations of skill and ardour. Absolon's skills are not best shown in playing Herod, and the offer of money would affront most women by its lack of tact.

Fro day to day this joly Absalon
So woweth hir, that him is wo bigon.
He waketh al the night and al the day; 265
He kempte hise lokkes brode, and made him gay;
He woweth hir by menes and brocage,
And swoor he wolde been hir owne page;
He singeth, brokkinge as a nightingale;
He sente hir piment, meeth, and spyced ale, 270
And wafres, pyping hote out of the glede;
And for she was of toune, he profred mede.
For som folk wol ben wonnen for richesse,
And som for strokes, and som for gentillesse.
Somtyme, to shewe his lightnesse and maistrye, 275
He pleyeth Herodes on a scaffold hye.
But what availleth him as in this cas?
She loveth so this hende Nicholas,
That Absolon may blowe the bukkes horn;
He ne hadde for his labour but a scorn; 280
And thus she maketh Absolon hir ape,
And al his ernest turneth til a jape.

264–6   *So woweth hir . . . made him gay*: he courts her to distraction. Loss of sleep was an 'official' symptom of love – we notice his personal vanity still comes first, and he spends much time on his hair and beautifying himself.

267   *menes and brocage*: the words survive in modern 'means and brokerage' – both imply an intermediary. This may mean he got others to plead his cause, or simply that he sent messages and gifts by servants.

269   *He singeth, brokkinge as a nightingale*: 'He sings in a quavering tone like the nightingale.'

270–72   *He sent hir piment . . . he profred mede*: his gifts are rather prosaic: two sorts of drink made of honey, ale spiced up (spices were costly), cakes piping hot from the oven – and, 'because she lived in a town', money. There were very few shops as we understand them where one could buy personal trinkets and the like, which were sold by travelling pedlars: only in the more prosperous towns were there permanent places run entirely on a cash basis. There was very little money in circulation – much buying was done on credit, and poor people probably used a good deal of barter. Most modern girls – however flighty – would be annoyed to be offered cash, because the implication of prostitution is too obvious. It does not seem a tactful approach – and it is hard to see what she could have spent it on. Perhaps the key is in the word 'profred' – he tried to give her money but she declined it.

273–4   *For som folk . . . gentillesse*: 'For some people are overcome by wealth, some are conquered by rough treatment and some by good manners.' This topic – a sort of Medieval Guide to Success with Women – is discussed at length, and with much pungency, by the Wife of Bath. Nicholas, of course, combines some rather rough tactics with a lot of verbal 'gentillesse'.

275–6   *Somtyme . . . on a scaffold hye*: 'Sometimes, to show off his agile skill, he played the part of Herod on a scaffold erected' (in the street, where the Mystery plays were often performed). As Herod, like Pilate, was acted as a roaring, heavy villain, the slim-built, squeaky-voiced Absolon is an unlikely piece of casting.

279   *Absolon may blowe the bukkes horn*: 'Absolon can go chase himself.' The line is very colloquial.

Ful sooth is this proverbe, it is no lye,
Men seyn right thus, 'Alwey the nye slye
Maketh the ferre leve to be looth.'   285
For though that Absolon be wood or wrooth,
By-cause that he fer was from hir sighte,
This nye Nicholas stood in his lighte.
Now bere thee wel, thou hende Nicholas!
For Absolon may waille and singe 'Allas.'   290
And so bifel it on a Saterday,
This carpenter was goon til Osenay;
And hende Nicholas and Alisoun
Acorded been to this conclusioun,
That Nicholas shal shapen him a wyle   295
This sely jalous housbond to bigyle;
And if so be the game wente aright,
She sholde slepen in his arm al night,
For this was his desyr and hir also.
And right anon, with-outen wordes mo,   300
This Nicholas no lenger wolde tarie,
But doth ful softe un-to his chambre carie
Bothe mete and drinke for a day or tweye,
And to hir housbonde bad hir for to seye,
If that he axed after Nicholas,   305
She sholde seye she niste where he was,
Of al that day she saugh him nat with yë;
She trowed that he was in maladye,
For, for no cry, hir mayde coude him calle;
He nolde answere, for no-thing that mighte falle.   310
This passeth forth al thilke Saterday,
That Nicholas stille in his chambre lay,
And eet and sleep, or dide what him leste,
Til Sonday, that the sonne gooth to reste.

284–5 *Alwey the nye ... to be looth*: a proverb we have lost – 'The crafty one near at hand makes the distant beloved seem hateful.' We put it slightly differently: 'Out of sight, out of mind.'

287–8 *By-cause that he ... in his lighte*: the wording of the proverb is picked up and applied to the two men, aptly enough, since Absolon cannot easily speak to Alison directly, but Nicholas, who 'gets in his light', lives in the same house.

294 *Acorded been to this conclusioun*: 'agreed on this plan'.

295 *shapen*: 'plan' or 'arrange'. In the north people still speak of 'framing themselves' to do something.

296 *sely*: 'simple' and also 'devout'. He was both, in his way.

299 *For this was his desyr and hir also*: we note that they *both* wanted this – there is no shy maiden being seduced here.

302 *softe*: 'secretly'.

303 *mete*: 'meat' means, as it still does in northern speech, food generally.

306 *niste*: 'ne wiste' – 'did not know'.

307–8 *Of al that day ... he was in maladye*: 'She had not set eyes on him all day and believed he was ill.'

311 *This passeth forth al thilke Saterday*: 'This went on all through that Saturday'.

The last major character is introduced – again by a different method. The Carpenter is brought alive almost entirely by the way in which he speaks. Garrulous, opinionated and full of platitudes, he bears all the marks of age and simplicity.

This sely carpenter hath greet merveyle   315
Of Nicholas, or what thing mighte him eyle,
And seyde, 'I am adrad, by seint Thomas,
It stondeth nat aright with Nicholas.
God shilde that he deyde sodeynly!
This world is now ful tikel, sikerly;   320
I saugh to-day a cors y-born to chirche
That now, on Monday last, I saugh him wirche.
Go up,' quod he un-to his knave anoon,
'Clepe at his dore, or knokke with a stoon,
Loke how it is, and tel me boldely.'   325
This knave gooth him up ful sturdily,
And at the chambre-dore, whyl that he stood,
He cryde and knokked as that he were wood: –
'What! how! what do ye, maister Nicholay?
How may ye slepen al the longe day?'   330
But al for noght, he herde nat a word;
An hole he fond, ful lowe up-on a bord,
Ther as the cat was wont in for to crepe;
And at that hole he looked in ful depe,
And at the laste he hadde of him a sighte.   335
This Nicholas sat gaping ever up-righte,
As he had kyked on the newe mone.
Adoun he gooth, and tolde his maister sone
In what array he saugh this ilke man.

315–16 *This sely carpenter ... might him eyle*: 'This simple carpenter wondered greatly about Nicholas, or what was wrong with him.'

317 *I am adrad, by seint Thomas*: 'I am afraid, by Thomas à Becket' – perhaps the most famous saint England could boast at that time, and, of course, very apt here, as it is to his shrine at Canterbury that the pilgrimage is made.

319 *Gold shilde that he deyde sodeynly*: 'God forbid that he should suddenly die!'

320 *tikel*: 'hair-trigger', later to be called 'tickle of the sere', which conveys the sense. In those days death was always just around the corner – plague, accidents which would now be minor but were then fatal, made life extremely uncertain. The Carpenter's wise words are, in fact, what everyone knew perfectly well. That he had seen a man working last Monday and carried to his burial today (Saturday) would be nothing remarkable.

323 *knave*: the 'knave', or boy, makes the tally of servants (with the 'mayde') complete.

324–6 *Clepe at his dore ... ful sturdily*: 'clepe' was to call, both in the sense of calling a person by name and here calling out; to knock with a stone suggests serious measures. That the lad should tell him 'boldly' what he found, and that he goes to the room 'sturdily', implies some fear of dreadful discovery.

329 *maister*: a polite title. It is not clear whether Nicholas has even graduated, let alone proceeded to the Master of Arts degree from which this – and modern Mister – derive.

332–3 *An hole he fond ... for to crepe*: a delightful domestic touch. Cats were esteemed in the Middle Ages, when wooden houses were plagued with rats and mice. As most interior walls were of lath, it was easy to make pop-holes so that the cats could go freely from room to room and keep down the vermin.

335 *at the laste he hadde of him a sighte*: 'finally he caught a glimpse of him'.

336 *This Nicholas sat gaping ever up-righte*: 'Nicholas sat all the time bolt upright with his mouth open.'

337 *As he had kyked on the newe mone*: 'as if he had peeped at the new moon'. This was supposed to be dangerous to one's sanity. We still have residual superstitions about the new moon – seeing it through glass, for instance, is unlucky to some people, and a nonsense-invocation, 'White Rabbits!', has to be said. Compare this with the 'night-spel' at l. 372.

339 *In what array he saugh this ilke man*: 'In what condition he saw this very man.' Nicholas has chosen an effective ploy – total silence and apparent paralysis of all the faculties. This is as intriguing as it is impressive.

The Carpenter's character is now more fully developed. He distrusts learning and believes in the wisdom of the plain, uneducated man that he sees in himself. He has a simple piety – expressed in his invocation of the saints, which is not mere blasphemy – and he also shows some signs of how he came to be so successful in his own trade: when it comes to giving orders to deal with a problem that lies within his own competence, the removal of a door, he is brisk and efficient.

This carpenter to blessen him bigan,	340
And seyde, 'Help us, seinte Frideswyde!	
A man woot litel what him shal bityde.	
This man is falle, with his astromye,	
In som woodnesse or in som agonye;	
I thoghte ay wel how that it sholde be!	345
Men sholde nat knowe of goddes privetee.	
Ye, blessed be alwey a lewed man,	
That noght but only his bileve can!	
So ferde another clerk with astromye;	
He walked in the feeldes for to prye	350
Up-on the sterres, what ther sholde bifalle,	
Til he was in a marle-pit y-falle;	
He saugh nat that. But yet, by seint Thomas,	
Me reweth sore of hende Nicholas.	
He shal be rated of his studying,	355
If that I may, be Jesus, hevene king!	
Get me a staf, that I may underspore,	
Whyl thou, Robin, hevest up the dore.	
He shal out of his studying, as I gesse' –	
And to the chambre-dore he gan him dresse.	360

340   *blessen him*: 'to sign himself with the cross'.

341   *seinte Frideswyde*: Saint Frideswide is interesting as a 'local' saint: she had a shrine from the eighth century round which Oxford grew up – a tablet in Christ Church records this. The Carpenter is a devout man in his simple way, and this is to be taken as prayer, not blasphemy.

343–4   *This man is falle ... in som agonye*: 'Through dabbling in astronomy this man has fallen into some mental or physical illness.' The carpenter's distrust of learning rather than secret arts is the important point here.

345   *I thoghte ay wel how that it sholde be!*: a nice character-line – 'I always knew how it would turn out!'

346   *goddes privetee*: the concept of God's secret purposes is to play an important role in what follows.

347   *lewed*: 'lewd' now means 'crude', 'dirty-minded', but originally just 'uneducated'.

348   *noght but only his bileve can*: 'can' is used here, as often, in the sense of know; 'bileve' is the Creed, which we so call from its opening in Latin – '*Credo* in unum Deum' – 'I *believe* in one God'. This prayer embodies the basic tenets of Christianity: the Carpenter would know it by heart, together with his Paternoster and Ave Maria (Lord's Prayer and Hail Mary), and felt that that was enough for any man.

349   *So ferde another clerk with astromye*: 'So it happened to another student with his astromy' – the last word is presumably an ignorant blunder for the proper term.

352   *in a marle-pit y-falle*: the student so intent on reading the future in the stars that he fell into a marl-pit would have a sticky end, as marl is a clay, often then dug out and worked into the land because it had a high lime content.

353   *by seint Thomas*: the Carpenter calls on a saint appropriate in another way – Thomas à Becket, to whose shrine the pilgrims are riding.

354–5   *Me reweth sore ... of his studying*: a further touch of character – the Carpenter is genuinely worried about Nicholas, it appears, and at the same time is sure he can scold him out of his foolish studies.

357–8   *Get me a staf ... hevest up the dore*: brisk instructions in practical affairs suggest his own calling. To underspore is to lever – most hinges then were of the ring and peg variety: the Miller himself could lift barn doors off their hinges.

His knave was a strong carl for the nones,
And by the haspe he haf it up atones;
In-to the floor the dore fil anon.
This Nicholas sat ay as stille as stoon,
And ever gaped upward in-to the eir.   365
This carpenter wende he were in despeir,
And hente him by the sholdres mightily,
And shook him harde, and cryde spitously,
'What! Nicholay! what, how! what! loke adoun!
Awake, and thenk on Cristes passioun;   370
I crouche thee from elves and fro wightes!'
Ther-with the night-spel seyde he anon-rightes
On foure halves of the hous aboute,
And on the threshfold of the dore with-oute: –
'Jesu Crist, and sëynt Benedight,   375
Blesse this hous from every wikked wight,
For nightes verye, the white *paternoster*! –
Where wentestow, seynt Petres soster?'

Having seen Nicholas as a seducer, we now see him as a confidence-trickster. The deception of the Carpenter is handled with great skill, from the dramatic moment when he first speaks, to the astounding declaration that everyone is to die: the story is supported by strong drink and the supposition that it is told in strictest confidence – a good formula in any circumstances.

361   *for the nones*: often means little; here 'for the job he had to do' would render the sense, literally 'for the occasion'.

364   *stille as stoon*: a stock phrase.

366–7   *This carpenter wende ... by the sholdres mightily*: 'The Carpenter believed he was in a desperate state and grasped him powerfully by the shoulders.' 'Despair' often had a theological sense – despair in God's goodness, so belief in certain damnation. This is probably why the Carpenter urges him to think of Christ's death (l. 370) – which was to redeem mankind.

371–8   *I crouche thee ... seynt Petres soster*: this passage bristles with difficulties which learned comments often make more obscure. The first line states the purpose – 'I protect you with the sign of the cross from elves and other creatures!' The carpenter thinks evil forces have possessed his guest, and then goes on to utter a formula to protect the house at night-time, addressing it to the four quarters of the compass and the doorway. The 'night-spel' (l. 372) begins as a simple prayer and degenerates into what is almost certainly comical rubbish (ll. 375–8) – 'May Jesus and Saint Benedict keep this house safe from every evil creature – the White Paternoster against wicked spirits of the night – where did you get to, Saint Peter's sister?' That white is good and a 'black' form of the Lord's Prayer was used in magic is a little help: but though Saint Peter keeps the keys of Heaven, his sister is unrecorded. This sounds like one of the many mildly funny stories about children who get mixed up in their prayers.

And atte laste this hende Nicholas
Gan for to syke sore, and seyde, 'Allas!   380
Shal al the world be lost eftsones now?'
This carpenter answerde, 'What seystow?
What! thenk on god, as we don, men that swinke.'
This Nicholas answerde. 'Fecche me drinke;
And after wol I speke in privetee   385
Of certeyn thing that toucheth me and thee;
I wol telle it non other man, certeyn.'
This carpenter goth doun, and comth ageyn,
And broghte of mighty ale a large quart;
And whan that ech of hem had dronke his part,   390
This Nicholas his dore faste shette,
And doun the carpenter by him he sette.
He seyde, 'John, myn hoste lief and dere,
Thou shalt up-on thy trouthe swere me here,
That to no wight thou shalt this conseil wreye;   395
For it is Cristes conseil that I seye,
And if thou telle it man, thou are forlore;
For this vengaunce thou shalt han therefore,
That if thou wreye me, thou shalt be wood!'
'Nay, Crist forbede it, for his holy blood!'   400
Quod tho this sely man, 'I nam no labbe,
Ne, though I seye, I nam nat lief to gabbe.
Sey what thou wolt, I shal it never telle
To child ne wyf, by him that harwed helle!'
'Now, John,' quod Nicholas, 'I wol nat lye;   405
I have y-founde in myn astrologye,
As I have loked in the mone bright,
That now, a Monday next, at quarter-night,

380–81   *Allas! ... eftsones now*: a dramatic opening – and effective in a day when the Church was always preaching the nearness of death and judgement.

383   *swinke*: 'labour'. Men that labour are obviously sensible!

385   *privetee*: the key to what follows. Men are not supposed to know God's plans, and if one of them is entrusted with this special knowledge it must be kept secret. This is emphasized a moment later (l. 387) – 'I will certainly not tell it to any other man but you'.

389   *mighty ale*: small beer was made for everyday use, strong (or 'mighty') ale was kept for special occcasions. As they split a generous quart of this potent stuff, the Carpenter is probably more easy to manipulate.

393–5   *John, myn hoste ... conseil wreye*: a tone both confidential and intimate is adopted now – 'John, my very dear host, you (he uses the familiar singular, 'thou') must give me your word that you won't betray this secret to any man because it is Christ's confidence that I am telling you.'

397–9   *And if thou telle ... thou shalt be wood*: the intriguing bait of being in on God's secrets – and being the only man to share them – is followed up by awesome threats: if the Carpenter betrays what he is to hear, he is damned – he will be driven mad as (divine) punishment for being false to Nicholas.

400   *Nay, Crist forbede it, for his holy blood*: as we have seen already, the Carpenter is a garrulous man, with his anecdotes of marl-pits and his repeated, simplistic opinions. Such men are usually sure of their own reticence and secrecy.

401–2   *labbe ... gabbe*: words whose sense is apparent by their sound. The former means a tell-tale, the latter a chatterer. To gab, meaning to gossip, survives in some local dialects – and we still have a near equivalent of 'though I seye' – though I say it myself.

404   *by him that harwed helle*: 'by Christ' (who, according to medieval legend, went to Hell to rescue all those who could not have been Christians because they were born too early; his revelation of himself allowed them release). A harrow separates weeds from good soil.

408   *a Monday next, at quarter-night*: note the precise detail which supports the lie: 'this very next Monday, a quarter of the way through the night'. As Nicholas had stayed in his room all through Saturday, this appears to be taking place on Sunday: the flood is due tomorrow, it seems. As the night was conventionally from 6 p.m. to 6 a.m., the time suggested is about nine.

Shal falle a reyn and that so wilde and wood,
That half so greet was never Noës flood.   410
This world,' he seyde, 'in lasse than in an hour
Shal al be dreynt, so hidous is the shour;
Thus shal mankynde drenche and lese hir lyf.'

Nicholas now introduces material that would be familiar – and funny
– to the medieval listener. Noah's flood had acquired a number of additional details to those given in the Bible in the stories and plays of the
period: in particular, emphasis had been laid on the role of his wife – either
a shrewish woman who scolded him for messing about with boats instead
of getting on with his work, or an insatiably inquisitive wife who would
not rest until she knew the reason for his new activity – and on the secrecy
which he was supposed to observe, keeping his intentions from everyone
else. What follows is clearly a parodic version of this tale.

This carpenter answerde, 'Allas, my wyf!
And shal she drenche? Allas! myn Alisoun!'   415
For sorwe of this he fil almost adoun,
And seyde, 'Is ther no remedie in this cas?'
'Why, yis, for gode,' quod hende Nicholas,
'If thou wolt werken after lore and reed;
Thou mayst nat werken after thyn owene heed.   420
For thus seith Salomon, that was ful trewe,
"Werk al by conseil, and thou shalt nat rewe."
And if thou werken wolt by good conseil,
I undertake, with-outen mast and seyl,
Yet shal I saven hir and thee and me.   425
Hastow nat herd how saved was Noë,
Whan that our lord had warned him biforn
That al the world with water sholde be lorn?'
'Yis,' quod this carpenter, 'ful yore ago.'
'Hastow nat herd,' quod Nicholas, 'also   430
The sorwe of Noë with his felawshipe,
Er that he mighte gete his wyf to shipe?
Him had be lever, I dar wel undertake,
At thilke tyme, than alle his wetheres blake,
That she hadde had a ship hir-self allone.   435
And ther-fore, wostou what is best to done?
This asketh haste, and of an hastif thing
Men may nat preche or maken tarying.

410   *Noës flood*: the story of Noah's flood was much preached upon and used in the Mystery plays. It was closely associated with the idea of the Last Day.

411–13   *This world ... lese hir lyf*: the downpour (much more than a 'shower') will be so fearsome that everything will be under water in an hour and the whole human race drowned and dead.

414   *Allas, my wyf!*: it is ironic and touching that the Carpenter's first thought is for the safety of his wife.

417–19   *Is ther no remedie ... lone and reed*: 'Is there no solution to this problem?' 'Yes, by God (*or*, there is a good one, depending on the use of a capital in the text), if you will act on my advice and instructions.'

421   *Salomon*: medieval for Solomon. Nicholas appears to be playing tricks with his text (l. 422) – 'Do all things by advice and you shall not regret it' is apparently the reference, and this is from Ecclesiasticus, not Proverbs.

424   *I undertake, with-outen mast and seyl*: 'I guarantee, without mast or sail' – that is, they will not need to have a proper boat.

429   *ful yore ago*: the Carpenter says that he heard the story of Noah a long time ago, which probably means he has known it all his life rather than that he has only a distant memory of it. Noah was a favourite subject, as we have said, for sermons on such things as Being Prepared for the Worst, and the legends that had grown up about his wife provided material for sermons on the untrustworthy nature of the daughters of Eve – she was supposed to have tried to wriggle the secret of the Ark out of him – or the meddlesome nature of women – she was supposed to have opposed the whole idea and made great difficulties about going on board. This made for some crudely amusing drama. Nicholas pursues the second idea, but perhaps the first one would be in the minds of the audience, as this Noah's wife is very untrustworthy indeed.

430–32   *Hastow nat herd ... wyf to shipe*: 'Haven't you heard the trouble Noah and his family had to get her to go on board?' Nicholas is making it easy for Alison to play her part – she will be able to act out surprise and protest, being warned of this.

433–4   *Him had be lever ... his wetheres blake*: constructions with 'lever' were common but sound odd to us: the literal sense is 'It would be dearer to him' where we should say 'He would rather she'd had a ship to herself on that occasion than (keep) all his black sheep.' Why black ones were valuable to him is not clear.

438   *Men may nat preche or maken tarying*: 'You can't hang about making a sermon of it.'

Anon go gete us faste in-to this in
A kneding-trogh, or elles a kimelin,   440
For ech of us, but loke that they be large,
In whiche we mowe swimme as in a barge,
And han ther-inne vitaille suffisant
But for a day; fy on the remenant!
The water shal aslake and goon away   445
Aboute pryme up-on the nexte day.
But Robin may nat wite of this, thy knave,
Ne eek thy mayde Gille I may nat save;
Axe nat why, for though thou aske me,
I wol nat tellen goddes privetee.   450
Suffiseth thee, but if thy wittes madde,
To han as greet a grace as Noë hadde.
Thy wyf shal I wel saven, out of doute,
Go now thy wey, and speed thee heeraboute.
But whan thou hast, for hir and thee and me,   455
Y-geten us thise kneding-tubbes three,
Than shaltow hange hem in the roof ful hye,
That no man of our purveyaunce spye.
And whan thou thus hast doon as I have seyd,
And hast our vitaille faire in hem y-leyd,   460
And eek an ax, to smyte the corde atwo
When that the water comth, that we may go,
And broke an hole an heigh, up-on the gable,
Unto the gardin-ward, over the stable,
That we may frely passen forth our way   465
Whan that the grete shour is goon away –
Than shaltow swimme as myrie, I undertake,
As doth the whyte doke after hir drake.
Than wol I clepe, "How! Alison! How! John!
Be myrie, for the flood wol passe anon."   470
And thou wolt seyn, "Hayl, maister Nicholay!
Good morwe, I se thee wel, for it is day."
And than shul we be lordes al our lyf
Of al the world, as Noë and his wyf.

439   *in*: he calls the house an inn, but probably not in any technical sense – just a dwelling.

440   *A kneding-trogh, or elles a kimelin*: two regular jobs in medieval households were baking bread for the week and brewing light beer – often done together when the kitchen was warm: so large tubs for kneading dough, and kimelins, brewing-tubs, were common articles.

442   *barge*: 'barge' does not imply a narrow canal freighter, but a stately vessel.

444   *fy on the remenant*: colloquial – 'to blazes with the rest!'

446   *pryme*: Prime was the first of the six Day Hours of the strict monastic life: it was and is sung at about six in the morning, and re-creates the reviling of Christ after capture on Good Friday. In medieval England one was never far from the sound of church or monastery bells, and these served as rough indicators of the time.

447   *knave*: 'boy', as in modern German. The Carpenter had a strong lad to help about the house, and a girl, presumably to act as Alison's maid and to do other domestic duties.

451–2   *Suffiseth thee ... as Noë hadde*: 'Unless you are crazy it should be enough for you to be shown as much mercy as Noah was.' Noah was saved, but in the medieval mind he also had an unhappy domestic life.

457   *in the roof ful hye*: 'high up in the attic or loft'.

458   *That no man of our purveyaunce spye*: 'so that no man can see what provision we are making' – the constant emphasis on secrecy is important in convincing the man.

460   *faire ... y-leyd*: 'properly stowed'.

461   *an ax*: the axe is to be important. A deluge which drowns the world in an hour will be a heavy one, so they must be ready for an instant getaway. The actual results of this detail are somewhat unexpected.

463–4   *up-on the gable ... gardin-ward*: the gable wall may well be little more than lath and clay, so to break through it would be easy. It is a nice touch to insist that the hole should be facing the garden ('-ward' could be added to words. as we still say 'homeward') as it emphasizes yet again the necessity for absolute secrecy. Nicholas does not want the old man talking to anyone about this plan.

468   *As doth the whyte doke after hir drake*: a delightful picture, and quite a subtle joke, since it makes the Carpenter into a duck, not a drake: he is to lose his male rights.

471   *And thou wolt seyn ... Of al the world*: a charming picture is vividly drawn of them all floating along happily, calling to each other - and it is spiced with a taste of power With everyone dead, they will rule the world.

Nicholas now introduces the idea of passing the night in celibacy – indeed, the Carpenter must sleep well away from Alison in case he even thinks a sinful thought. This arrangement is very convenient for the purpose he has in mind, and would not seem strange to Chaucer's audience. Indeed, in Russia, as late as 1900, the idea of keeping oneself 'pure' on the eve of any important occasion was strong enough for there to be general disapproval of any child born on Christmas Day – since, in theory, this meant its parents had made love on the night of Lady Day, one of the great church festivals, 25 March.

But of o thyng I warne thee ful right, 475
Be wel avysed, on that ilke night
That we ben entred in-to shippes bord,
That noon of us ne speke nat a word,
Ne clepe, ne crye, but been in his preyere;
For it is goddes owne heste dere. 480
Thy wyf and thou mote hange fer a-twinne,
For that bitwixe yow shal be no sinne
No more in looking than ther shal in dede;
This ordinance is seyd, go, god thee spede!
Tomorwe at night, whan men ben alle aslepe, 485
In-to our kneding-tubbes wol we crepe,
And siten ther, abyding goddes grace.
Go now thy wey, I have no lenger space
To make of this no lenger sermoning.
Men seyn thus, "Send the wyse, and sey no-thing;" 490
Thou art so wys, it nedeth thee nat teche;
Go, save our lyf, and that I thee biseche.'
This sely carpenter goth forth his wey.
Ful ofte he seith 'Allas' and 'Weylawey,'
And to his wyf he tolde his privetee; 495
And she was war, and knew it bet than he,
What al this queynte cast was for to seye.
But nathelees she ferde as she wolde deye,
And seyde, 'Allas! go forth thy wey anon,
Help us to scape, or we ben lost echon; 500

475–84 *But of o thyng . . . This ordinance is seyd*: 'But I warn you strictly
about one thing – on that very night that we go on board, be most
careful that nobody calls or says anything aloud except in prayer;
for it is God's special command – and your wife and you must hang
well apart so that there is no sexual sin between you, not in looking any
more than in action. This is decreed.' Ostensibly the silence is for
secrecy and the celibacy is because they are about God's purposes and
must be chaste: Nicholas does not want the carpenter chattering half
the night away, or staying awake fancying his wife.

487 *abyding goddes grace*: 'waiting on the mercy of God'.

490 *Send the wyse, and sey no-thing*: a nice piece of flattery. We have
already seen that the Carpenter esteems himself a wise man, in spite of
his lack of education – indeed, he thinks education is downright
dangerous. So now Nicholas plays on his vanity with a proverbial
phrase – 'Send a sensible man to do something and he needs no
instructions.' In modern English we still say 'A word to the wise is
enough', which is from an old Latin proverb, *Verbum sapientia sat est*.
Chaucer might actually have had this phrase in mind.

491 *Thou art so wys, it nedeth thee nat teche*: 'You are so wise you don't
need to be taught anything.' The flattery becomes outrageous here.
Nicholas is sure he has his man. He has already trodden on some very
thin ice in talking about the mercy or grace of God which they are all
to await – in view of what we know he and Alison are expecting, this
is blasphemous.

494 *Ful ofte he seith 'Allas' and 'Weylawey'*: conventional expressions of
grief, like cries for help (the 'Harrow!' that Alison threatened to utter
but didn't), are not easy to translate 'He often said "O dear me" ' is near
enough. The Carpenter does not use strong language.

495 *privetee*: the famous word occurs again, with its sexual overtones.

496–8 *And she was war . . . she wolde deye*: 'And she understood even
better than he did what this extraordinary plan meant, but nevertheless
behaved as if she were going to die' (of shock or fear). Chaucer gets
another improper pun on the word 'queynte', which had an anatomical
meaning that is obviously relevant here. The 'cast' or plot is to secure
sexual pleasure, as she knows and her husband does not. As he dotes
on her, her fearful urging prompts him to great – and tiring – efforts,
all part of the plan.

500 *echon*: 'all of us', literally 'each one'. This sense of 'lost' is still used
in 'lost at sea' and similar phrases.

I am thy trewe verray wedded wyf;
Go, dere spouse, and help to save our lyf.
Lo! which a greet thing is affeccioun!
Men may dye of imaginacioun,
So depe may impressioun be take.   505
This sely carpenter biginneth quake;
Him thinketh verraily that he may see
Noës flood come walwing as the see
To drenchen Alisoun, his hony dere.
He wepeth, weyleth, maketh sory chere,   510
He syketh with ful many a sory swogh.

The development of the plot here is skilful because the groundwork for
it has been unobtrusively laid long before. The Carpenter is a master of
his craft; he is also a fusspot, and he has been especially cautioned that
no one must know what he is doing. Thus he busies himself making
ladders – a skilled task – preparing the vessels, provisioning and hanging
them and making arrangements for his servants to go on a spurious
errand. After so much effort and anxiety, the old man is worn out, and
needs no sleeping-draught to keep him quiet while his wife and Nicholas
enjoy themselves.

He gooth and geteth him a kneding-trogh,
And after that a tubbe and a kimelin,
And prively he sente hem to his in,
And heng hem in the roof in privetee.   515
His owne hand he made laddres three,
To climben by the ronges and the stalkes
Un-to the tubbes hanginge in the balkes,
And hem vitailled, bothe trogh and tubbe,
With breed and chese, and good ale in a jubbe,   520
Suffysinge right y-nogh as for a day.
But er that he had maad al this array,
He sente his knave, and eek his wenche also,
Up-on his nede to London for to go.
And on the Monday, whan it drow to night,   525
He shette his dore with-oute candel-light,

501   *I am thy trewe verray wedded wyf*: a highly ironic line.

503–5   *which a greet thing ... impressioun be take*: Chaucer's English was not yet well adapted to express abstract concepts, which were still usually presented in Latin. Here he exclaims that our fancy is so powerful that men may even die of it, it can so impress itself upon us. 'Affeccioun' may be translated as 'emotion', but this does not easily match the 'imaginacioun' of the next line, and is, in any case, a very vague word.

507   *Him thinketh*: a typical impersonal form – where we should say 'he thought', medieval construction favoured the oblique 'it was thought to him'.

508   *come walwing as the see*: 'come rolling in like the sea' – 'walwing' is very expressive in sound.

511   *He syketh with ful many a sory swogh*: with its heavy alliteration, this line is more like a piece of Anglo-Saxon poetry than medieval – Chaucer does sometimes revert to this traditional form for a special, strong effect. Literally, 'he sighs with many a sorry sigh'.

516   *His owne hand he made laddres three*: 'With his own hands he made three ladders.' This, of course, would be one of the proper range of accomplishments for a master carpenter – and he is not going to get an assistant to do it because of the strict injunctions he has had about 'privetee'.

517   *the ronges and the stalkes*: the technical terms for the parts of a ladder are rungs and stiles. We might find it simpler to call the latter uprights.

518   *balkes*: the rafters of the house from which the vessels have been slung by ropes.

520   *jubbe*: 'jug'. The ale is presumably of the better quality referred to earlier.

521   *Suffysinge right y-nogh as for a day*: 'amply sufficient for a day'.

523–4   *He sente his knave ... to London for to go*: Nicholas had advised him that his servants could not be saved – of course he wants everyone who might tell tales out of the house – so the Carpenter sends them on an errand ('up-on his nede') to London, a considerable journey. Depending on the mode of travel, it could well take them a week to get there and back.

526   *He shette his dore with-oute candel-light*: 'He secured his door without showing (or using) a light.' This is all part of the secrecy which he supposes so important, but it has other repercussions in the story – it helps Absolon to come to the conclusion that the house is empty except for Alison.

And dressed al thing as it sholde be.
And shortly, up they clomben alle three;
They sitten stille wel a furlong-way.
'Now, *Pater-noster*, clom!' seyde Nicholay,   530
And 'Clom!' quod John, and 'Clom!' seyde Alisoun.
This carpenter seyde his devocioun,
And stille he sit, and biddeth his preyere,
Awaytinge on the reyn, if he it here.
The dede sleep, for wery bisinesse,   535
Fil on this carpenter right, as I gesse,
Aboute corfew-tyme, or litel more;
For travail of his goost he groneth sore,
And eft he routeth, for his heed mislay.
Doun of the laddre stalketh Nicholay,   540
And Alisoun, ful softe adoun she spedde;
With-outen wordes mo, they goon to bedde
Ther-as the carpenter is wont to lye.
Ther was the revel and the melodye;
And thus lyth Alison and Nicholas,   545
In bisinesse of mirthe and of solas,

527   *And dressed al thing as it sholde be*: 'And he arranged everything properly.'

529   *They sitten stille wel a furlong-way*: literally, 'They sat still for a good furlong-length.' A furlong, an old land-measurement still used by some country folk, is an eighth of a mile. It is based on the word furrow, and was the traditional length of a ploughing-strip in the large open fields of medieval villages. Ploughing with oxen, which go at about two miles an hour, a furrow took nearly four minutes to cut. It thus became a handy indication of a short space of time in an age that had no watches – we might say they sat for a good five minutes.

530   *Now*, Pater-noster, *clom!*: this is very homely – 'Now Our Father and shurrup!' Nicholas is making a mere token prayer. The Carpenter, as we have seen, is more devout.

532–3   *This carpenter seyde ... biddeth his preyere*: 'The carpenter said his own prayer and sits still telling his beads.' 'To bid' originally meant 'to pray' (as in our Bidding Prayer) and because beads were used as a help to prayer, the sense became transferred to the object. 'Biddeth' suggests that he is using his rosary as he waits.

535   *The dede sleep, for wery bisinesse*: we now understand why Nicholas had urged secrecy and speed on him: he has had to do everything himself, even to making the ladders, so no wonder that tiring exertions ('wery bisinesse') send him to sleep.

537   *corfew-tyme*: curfew, from 'couvre-feu', 'cover-fire', was an old safety regulation in those days of wood and thatch. As dark fell a bell was rung to warn householders to cover naked flames and put out their fires.

538–9   *For travail ... his heed mislay*: 'Because he was so distressed in mind he groaned deeply, and he snored too because his head was lying crookedly.' These details are important to the story – there is no doubt that he is soundly off, and though Alison and Nicholas are quiet they can feel safe.

543   *Ther-as the carpenter is wont to lye*: 'where the carpenter usually slept'. There would be only one double bed in the house, in all probability, but this detail does rather emphasize the cuckoldry: the marriage-bed itself is used

544   *Ther was the revel and the melodye*: 'There they made sweet music together'.

546   *In bisinesse of mirthe and of solas*: 'busy enjoying themselves'.

Til that the belle of laudes gan to ringe,
And freres in the chauncel gonne singe.

    The re-introduction of Absolon at this point serves a double purpose.
It begins a new theme – that of the kissing at the window and its various
consequences – and also draws our interest away from one of the major
characters. We are soon so engrossed in the antics of the young that we
forget the old man snoring away in the rafters – until the climax of the
story.

This parish-clerk, this amorous Absolon,
That is for love alwey so wo bigon,   550
Up-on the Monday was at Oseneye
With companye, him to disporte and pleye,
And axed up-on cas a cloisterer
Ful prively after John the carpenter;
And he drough him a-part out of the chirche,   555
And seyde, 'I noot, I saugh him here nat wirche
Sin Saterday; I trow that he be went
For timber, ther our abbot hath him sent;
For he is wont for timber for to go,
And dwellen at the grange a day or two;   560
Or elles he is at his hous, certeyn;
Wher that he be, I can nat sothly seyn.'
This Absolon ful joly was and light,
And thoghte, 'now is tyme wake al night;
For sikirly I saugh him nat stiringe   565
Aboute his dore sin day bigan to springe.
So moot I thryve, I shal, at cokkes crowe,
Ful prively knokken at his windowe
That stant ful lowe up-on his boures wal.
To Alison now wol I tellen al   570
My love-longing, for yet I shal nat misse
That at the leste wey I shal hir kisse.
Som maner confort shal I have, parfay,
My mouth hath icched al this longe day;
That is a signe of kissing atte leste.   575
Al night me mette eek, I was at a feste.
Therfor I wol gon slepe an houre or tweye,
And al the night than wol I wake and pleye.'

547 *laudes*: Lauds is sung immediately after the last of the Nocturns, which is sung at 4 a.m. It is a service heralding the dawn which shortly follows, and, as its name implies, it is principally a service of praise and joy. There is an echo of the 'melodye' that Alison and Nicholas have been so harmoniously making, though their joy is in the things of this world rather than the next.

548 *And freres in the chauncel gonne singe*: 'And friars go into the chancel to sing.' The chancel is the part of the church where the choir sits. Friars travelled, but they did have their 'houses', complete with chapels, where offices were sung as in monasteries.

553–5 *And axed up-on cas ... out of the chirche*: 'And happened to ask a monk (who was not supposed to leave the cloisters) confidentially about John the carpenter: and he (the monk) drew him (Absolon) aside out of the church.' Why he should do so is not clear, unless some service is in progress. The casual question can hardly have suggested anything suspicious.

556 *I noot*: a typical contraction: 'I ne woot', 'I don't know'.

557–8 *I trow ... hath him sent*: 'I imagine he has been sent to choose timber by the abbot.' As a master-carpenter, apparently with a regular contract at Osney, he would go and pick his own timber.

560 *grange*: a grange was usually a farm. Here perhaps a house in the country.

563 *ful joly was and light*: 'was cheerful and light-hearted'.

565–7 *For sikirly ... cokkes crowe*: the plot has worked – no one has seen the Carpenter all day – but this development was unexpected. Another reference is made to simple ways of telling time – cocks crow an hour or so before dawn.

572 *That at the leste wey I shal hir kisse*: 'so that I shall at least kiss her'. This is the first sign that this foolish youth has thought anything that could be called sexual.

574 *My mouth has icched al this longe day*: such superstitions still survive – if your palm itches, money is coming your way, for instance.

576 *Al night me mette eek, I was at a feste*: 'Also I dreamed all night I was at a feast.' One needs no Freud to interpret this dream.

578 *al the night than wol I wake and pleye*: 'Then all night I shall stay awake and enjoy myself.' 'Play' is ambiguous, simultaneously suggesting love-play and children's play.

Masterstudies: The Miller's Tale

The absurdity of Absolon's humiliation is strengthened by the careful preparations he makes. This time he is certain of some success, since the husband is apparently away. He makes himself smell nice, invokes the magical aid of a herb, and, above all, combs his crowning glory.

Whan that the firste cok hath crowe, anon
Up rist this joly lover, Absolon, 580
And him arrayeth gay, at point-devys.
But first he cheweth greyn and lycorys,
To smellen swete, er he had kembd his heer.
Under his tonge a trewe love he beer,
For ther-by wende he to ben gracious. 585
He rometh to the carpenteres hous,
And stille he stant under the shot-windowe;
Un-to his brest it raughte, it was so lowe;
And softe he cogheth with a semi-soun –
'What do ye, honey-comb, swete Alisoun? 590
My faire brid, my swete cinamome,
Awaketh, lemman myn, and speketh to me!
Wel litel thenken ye up-on my wo,
That for your love I swete ther I go.
No wonder is thogh that I swelte and swete; 595
I moorne as doth a lamb after the tete.
Y-wis, lemman, I have swich love-longinge,
That lyk a turtel trewe is my moorninge;
I may nat ete na more than a mayde.'
'Go fro the window, Jakke fool,' she sayde, 600
'As help me god, it wol nat be "Com ba me,"
I love another, and elles I were to blame,
Wel bet than thee, by Jesu, Absolon!
Go forth thy wey, or I wol caste a ston,

90

581–5   *And him arrayeth gay … to ben gracious*: a fine comic account of his preparations, with special attention to his crowning glory, his hair: 'He dressed himself up to the nines, but first chewed cardamon and liquorice to make himself fragrant – before he had combed his hair. He put a leaf of herb-paris under his tongue thinking to make himself agreeable.' This plant, *paris quadrifolia*, has four broad leaves: it was supposed to act as a sort of charm or love-philtre.

588   *Un-to his brest it raughte, it was so lowe*: 'It was so low down it reached to his chest.' The height of the window is important in the farcical action that follows.

589   *with a semi-soun*: literally 'with a half-voice', so 'softly'.

590–96   *What do ye … after the tete*: this is a rich comic passage. He begins by asking her what she is doing – we know very well what she is doing with Nicholas – and starts offering all the conventional tributes of devotion of the courtly lover, expressing his suffering for her. These are pitched at a ridiculously low level, however: to say that he swelters and sweats wherever he goes, for longing, is not very poetical. To say that he yearns for her like a lamb after its mother's udder is bizarre. Anyone who has heard a small lamb bleating and the deep-voiced ewe replying will see that the picture of him (remembering, too, his high voice) is absurd – and the picture of her as a mother sheep is not likely to strike her as complimentary. The childish nature of his approach to her is also emphasized.

597–9   *Y-wis, lemman … more than a mayde*: here he is on more conventional ground: 'Truly, sweetheart, I have such a desire for you that I grieve like a turtle-dove [which was supposed to mate for life and die if its partner died, of grief], I cannot eat more than a young girl.' Conventionally unmarried girls had tiny appetites and were meek – a favourite word – in demeanour. No doubt some of them had and were.

In view of the realistic exercises upon which his beloved is engaged, this speech could hardly be worse expressed or worse timed.

600   *Go fro the window, Jakke fool*: colloquial – 'Get away from the window, you silly ass!'

601–2   *As help me god … I were to blame*: 'So help me, it's not going to be a matter of "Come and kiss me" – I love someone else, and it would be very wrong if I didn't.' There is deliberate ambiguity here – the 'another' implies her husband, but is probably a sort of aside to the listening Nicholas.

And lat me slepe, a twenty devel wey!'   605
'Allas,' quod Absolon, 'and weylawey!
That trewe love was ever so yvel biset!
Than kisse me, sin it may be no bet,
For Jesus love and for the love of me.'
'Wiltow than go thy wey ther-with?' quod she.   610
'Ye, certes, lemman,' quod this Absolon.
'Thanne make thee redy,' quod she, 'I come anon;'
And un-to Nicholas she seyde stille,
'Now hust, and thou shalt laughen al thy fille.'
This Absolon doun sette him on his knees,   615
And seyde, 'I am a lord at alle degrees;
For after this I hope ther cometh more!
Lemman, thy grace, and swete brid, thyn ore!'
The window she undoth, and that in haste,
'Have do,' quod she, 'com of, and speed thee faste,   620
Leste that our neighebores thee espye.'
This Absolon gan wype his mouth ful drye;
Derk was the night as pich, or as the cole,
And at the window out she putte hir hole,
And Absolon, him fil no bet ne wers,   625
But with his mouth he kiste hir naked ers
Ful savourly, er he was war of this.
Abak he sterte, and thoghte it was amis,
For wel he wiste a womman hath no berd;
He felte a thing al rough and long y-herd,   630

605   *lat me slepe, a twenty devel way!*: 'Let me get to sleep and be damned to you!'

607   *That trewe love was ever so yvel biset!*: 'That ever faithful love should be so maltreated!' What follows suggests that Absolon is not quite such a fool as he has seemed: if he can get a kiss, as he later says, he may get more.

613   *stille*: 'quietly'. The presence of Nicholas, unknown to Absolon, is an important part of the scene.

615   *doun sette him on his knees*: he kneels, like a good lover, and because the window is so low.

616–18   *I am a lord ... thyn ore*: 'I am the king of the castle – because after this I hope more will follow [meaning more advanced love-making, not more kisses] – sweetheart, grant me your grace, dainty little bird, show me mercy!' This is the elevated language of the courtly lover. The high-flown style is a careful build-up for the very low – one might say fundamental – joke which is shortly to be played on him.

622–3   *This Absolon ... or as the cole*: further delightful anticipations are indicated: 'Absolon wiped his mouth completely dry' (perhaps the leaf under his tongue was giving him salivary problems). 'The night was a black as pitch or charcoal' (the coal of the period was rarely mineral).

625   *him fil no bet ne wers*: literally, 'neither better nor worse happened to him'. The force of the line here seems to be rather as if the author were saying 'To tell you the honest truth', since what now happens is rather blunt.

627   *Ful savourly*: it is also very funny. Before he knew what he was doing, he had kissed her 'ful savourly' – 'with relish'. Had he been in contact with what he expected, he might well have relished it.

628–30   *Abak he sterte ... long y-herd*: the humour of what follows depends not only on the rather crude physical ingredients, though in a knockabout way they are funny enough, but rather on the extra-ordinary naïvety of this young man who so fancies himself as a lover – though the more truthful state of affairs seems to be that he fancies himself. So, in l. 628, we are told he 'thought something was wrong'. The next line assures us that he knew women are not usually bearded, but it seems he is ignorant of the fact that we all have body-hair, and it takes him a moment to work out what has happened. It is implied, in what follows, that in his bewilderment he must have uttered his perplexity, since Nicholas apparently heard him saying something about a beard, and found it highly amusing.

And seyde, 'Fy! Allas! What have I do?'
'Tehee!' quod she, and clapte the window to;
And Absolon goth forth a sory pas.
'A berd, a berd!' quod hende Nicholas,
'By goddes *corpus*, this goth faire and weel!'   635
This sely Absolon herde every deel,
And on his lippe he gan for anger byte;
And to him-self he seyde, 'I shal thee quyte!'
Who rubbeth now, who froteth now his lippes
With dust, with sond, with straw, with clooth, with chippes,   640
But Absolon, that seith ful ofte, 'Allas!
My soule bitake I un-to Sathanas,
But me wer lever than al this toun,' quod he,
'Of this despyt awroken for to be!
Allas!' quod he, 'allas! I ne hadde y-bleynt!'   645
His hote love was cold and al y-queynt;
For fro that tyme that he had kiste hir ers,
Of paramours he sette nat a kers,
For he was heled of his maladye;
Ful ofte paramours he gan deffye,   650
And weep as dooth a child that is y-bete.

This marks the end of the 'romantic' Absolon, and the emergence of a new theme – revenge. Vanity often goes with viciousness, and what he proposes to do to Alison far exceeds any hurt his pride has suffered. The point of change is also marked by the late introduction of a new character – the smith, whose robust view of the world is in marked contrast with Absolon's mixture of naïvety and spite, a spite which is sharpened by the smith's rough humour.

A softe paas he wente over the strete
Un-til a smith men cleped daun Gerveys,
That in his forge smithed plough-harneys;
He sharpeth shaar and culter bisily.   655
This Absolon knokketh al esily,

633 *And Absolon goth forth a sory pas*: 'and Absolon left, walking miserably'.

634 *'A berd, a berd!' quod hende Nicholas*: Nicholas appears to have heard what Absolon thought.

635 *By goddes* corpus, *this goth faire and weel!*: 'By the body of God, this is turning out marvellously!' The use of the Latin *corpus* may imply that he is swearing by the sacred wafer, Corpus Christi, which in the Mass took upon itself identification with the real body of Christ.

638 *I shal thee quyte!*: 'I'll be revenged on you!'

638–40 *Who rubbeth now … with chippes*: Absolon's frantic scrubbing of his lips with anything that comes to hand is a marked contrast with his careful preparations and also emphasizes his over-fastidious nature. Reality has defiled him.

643–5 *But me wer lever … hadde y-bleynt!*: 'I'd sooner be revenged for this than own the whole of this town, may I be damned if I wouldn't … Oh dear! Why didn't I turn away!' There is a mixture of the vindictive and the plaintive here – the hurt child, in fact.

646 *y-queynt*: 'quenched'. But the word also had an anatomical sense, and it is with a queynt in that meaning that he has just been in contact.

648 *Of paramours he sette nat a kers*: 'He didn't give a damn for sweethearts.' 'Paramour' is a rather lofty word for 'lover', and reflects his disillusionment with the whole 'courtly' concept of love.

650 *Ful ofte paramours he gan deffye*: the theme is repeated: 'he repeatedly renounced lovers'.

651 *And weep as dooth a child that is y-bete*: the impression of his childishness is kept up – but he is to prove a very nasty child.

652 *softe paas*: 'gentle step'.

653 *daun*: a courtesy title, from the Latin for Master, which gives modern Mister: however, he may have been a master-smith.

654–5 *plough-harneys … shaar and culter*: some technical terms appear here. The coulter, as it is now spelt, is the 'cutter' which breaks the ground in front of the share which 'shears' it and turns it over in a furrow. In rough ground these quickly became blunt and ploughmen worked very early, so it is not unusual for the smith to be busy so soon, as his speciality is apparently 'plough-harneys', that is ploughing equipment. He is industriously sharpening these items.

656 *al esily*: 'gently'. Absolon does not want Alison to hear that he is about, and her house is only across the street.

And seyde, 'Undo, Gerveys, and that anon.
'What, who artow?' 'It am I, Absolon'
'What, Absolon! for Cristes swete tree,
Why ryse ye so rathe, ey, *ben'cite!*   660
What eyleth yow? Som gay gerl, god it woot,
Hath broght yow thus up-on the viritoot;
By sëynt Note, ye woot wel what I mene.'
This Absolon ne roghte nat a bene
Of al his pley, no word agayn he yaf;   665
He hadde more tow on his distaf
Than Gerveys knew, and seyde, 'Freend so dere,
That hote culter in the chimenee here,
As lene it me, I have ther-with to done,
And I wol bringe it thee agayn ful sone'   670
Gerveys answerde, 'Certes, were it gold,
Or in a poke nobles alle untold,
Thou sholdest have, as I am trewe smith;
Ey, Cristes foo! What wol ye do ther-with?'
'Ther-of,' quod Absolon, 'be as be may;   675
I shal wel telle it thee to-morwe day' –
And caughte the culter by the colde stele
Ful softe out at the dore he gan to stele,
And wente un-to the carpenteres wal.
He cogheth first, and knokketh ther-with-al   680
Upon the windowe, righte as he dide er.
This Alison answerde, 'Who is ther
That knokketh so? I warante it a theef.'
'Why, nay,' quod he, 'god woot, my swete leef,
I am thyn Absolon, my dereling!   685
Of gold,' quod he, 'I have thee broght a ring;
My moder yaf it me, so god me save,
Ful fyn it is, and ther-to wel y-grave;
This wol I yeve thee, if thou me kisse!'
This Nicholas was risen for to pisse,   690
And thoghte he wolde amenden al the jape,
He sholde kisse his ers er that he scape.
And up the windowe dide he hastily,
And out his ers he putteth prively
Over the buttok, to the haunche-bon;   695
And ther-with spak this clerk, this Absolon,
'Spek, swete brid, I noot nat wher thou art.'

659 *for Cristes swete tree*: the smith is hearty and blasphemous, swearing by the blessed cross ('sweet' because it bought our redemption).

660 *rathe*: 'early'. The word survived in poetical usage until the present century.

ben'cite: 'benedicite', 'bless us!'

661–3 *Som gay gerl ... what I mene*: the smith's heavy-handed joking is misapplied: 'Some fancy piece, god knows, has got you up and eager so early – by St Neot, you know what I mean!' 'Viritoot' is of unknown origin, but here seems to carry a sexual significance. St Neot, like St Frideswide, was a Saxon saint.

664–5 *This Absolon ... al his pley*: 'Absolon didn't give a damn for all his fooling.'

666–7 *He hadde more tow ... Than Gerveys knew*: Literally, 'He had more tow on his distaff [on which tow, the 'raw material' of linen, was spiked in order to spin it] than Gerveys knew about.' We might say he had 'more up his sleeve'.

668 *hote culter*: the coulter is hot because the smith has been working on it, and has stood it by the chimney to cool off.

672 *Or in a poke nobles alle untold*: 'or gold coins in a bag which have not even been counted' (a 'pig in a poke' is the obvious survival of this word).

673 *Thou sholdest have*: probably the smith is rather easy about lending things because he would be very strong and no one would get away with anything he lent them. There is also a contrast between his big-hearted attitude and Absolon's spiteful one.

675 *Ther-of ... be as be may*: 'As to that, let it be what it will' – a deliberately vague reply.

677 *stele*: a trap-word – it means 'handle'. Coulters are made of iron, not steel.

681 *righte as he dide er*: 'exactly as he did before'.

684 *my swete leef*: 'my precious darling'.

686–8 *Of gold ... wel y-grave*: Absolon hopes to appeal this time to her cupidity: the gold ring is an heirloom from his mother and it is richly engraved or decorated.

691 *And thoghte he wolde amenden al the jape*: 'and thought he would improve on the whole joke'.

695 *Over the buttok, to the haunche-bon*: 'past the buttocks, right up to the top of the hip-bone'. Every male reader will realize, with a sympathetic shudder, to what awful perils he is exposing his manhood, and how hard it will be for him to scramble back in when the coulter is applied.

This Nicholas anon leet flee a fart,
As greet as it had been a thonder-dent,
That with the strook he was almost y-blent;   700
And he was redy with his iren hoot,
And Nicholas amidde the ers he smoot.
Of gooth the skin an hande-brede aboute,
The hote culter brende so his toute,
And for the smert he wende for to dye.   705
As he were wood, for wo he gan to crye –
'Help! water! water! help, for goddes herte!'

If the story has been read aloud, as Chaucer meant it to be, this is
perhaps the most effective moment of all: the audience has become so
engrossed in the goings-on at the window that it has forgotten the
husband until, prompt on the cue of 'Water!', he enters the story again
with a thump.

This carpenter out of his slumber sterte,
And herde oon cryen 'Water' as he were wood,
And thoghte, 'Allas! Now comth Nowélis flood!'   710
He sit him up with-outen wordes mo,
And with his ax he smoot the corde a-two,
And doun goth al; he fond neither to selle,
Ne breed ne ale, til he cam to the selle
Up-on the floor; and ther aswowne he lay.   715
Up sterte hir Alison, and Nicholay,
And cryden 'Out' and 'Harrow' in the strete.
The neighebores, bothe smale and grete,
In ronnen, for to gauren on this man,
That yet aswowne he lay, bothe pale and wan;   720

698   *a fart*: we are reminded that the breaking of wind was one of the functions about which Absolon was unusually (for the times) squeamish. Insult upon insult is being offered him. His sweetheart's voice turns out to be a rude noise.

699   *thonder-dent*: 'thunder-stroke'. An impressive performance, especially as it seems to be at will, and possibly a hint to the more subtle reader that some sort of rain is likely to follow.

700   *That with the strook he was almost y-blent*: 'so that he (Absolon) was almost blinded by the blast'.

702–3   *And Nicholas ... an hande-brede aboute*: 'He hit Nicholas square in the backside – off flies the skin all round for the breadth of a hand.' A dramatic structure used here for a dramatic moment.

704   *toute*: 'rear-end', 'backside'; 'anus', for those who prefer medical terminology.

705   *And for the smert he wende for to dye*: 'He thought the pain was going to kill him.'

706–7   *As he were wood ... for goddes herte!*: 'He started screaming, as if he were crazy, "Help, water, water! For God's sake!"' Cold water is still a quick and simple remedy for a burn – but we have quite forgotten that someone else is expecting an alarm-call to do with water.

710   *And thoghte, 'Allas! Now comth Nowélis flood!'*: 'And thought, "Heavens! Here is Noah's flood!"' The form 'Nowélis' is probably, like the earlier 'astromie', an indication of the carpenter's ignorant speech.

712   *his ax*: the axe is a good example of the skill of this narrative – it was unobtrusively mentioned much earlier, but now its importance is clear: the carpenter must cut the rope instantly, and fall.

713–15   *And doun goth al ... aswowne he lay*: 'Down falls everything: he found no time to do any deals until he hit the boards of the ground floor, where he lay unconscious.' The literal sense is that he had no time to sell either bread or beer, which were, of course, the provisions he had with him in his tub.

716   *Up sterte hir Alison*: literally, 'Alyson got herself up hurriedly'.

717   *'Out' and 'Harrow'*: two traditional cries for help – Alison had threatened to raise this cry when Nicholas first assaulted her.

718   *bothe smale and grete*: refers to rank or wealth, not size – 'both high and low'.

719   *gauren*: 'gape' or 'stare'.

For with the fal he brosten hadde his arm;
But stonde he moste un-to his owne harm.
For whan he spak, he was anon bore doun
With hende Nicholas and Alisoun.
They tolden every man that he was wood, 725
He was agast so of 'Nowélis flood'
Thurgh fantasye, that of his vanitee
He hadde y-boght him kneding-tubbes three,
And hadde hem hanged in the roof above;
And that he preyed hem, for goddes love, 730
To sitten in the roof, *par companye.*

The element of brutality already noticed is continued in the injury received by the Carpenter; but the medieval attitude to pain was different from ours, and the amused response of the townspeople reflects it. It remains for the Miller to sum up his story which he does rather as if he were pointing a moral: and indeed the Carpenter is punished for his jealousy, Absolon deeply wounded in his vanity, Nicholas will sleep on his face for some weeks and only Alison has her cake and eats it – and who can begrudge so pretty a poppet her fling?

The folk gan laughen at his fantasye;
In-to the roof they kyken and they gape,
And turned al his harm un-to a jape.
For what so that this carpenter answerde, 735
It was for noght, no man his reson herde;
With othes grete he was so sworn adoun,
That he was holden wood in al the toun;
For every clerk anon-right heeld with other.
They seyde, 'The man is wood, my leve brother.' 740

721–2 *For with the fal ... his owne harm*: 'He had broken his arm with the fall, but he has to abide by the damage he has brought upon himself'. The broken arm is more serious than we might suppose: fracture of any major bone was dangerous in those days, he is no longer young, and as a working carpenter the injury will mean loss of income.

723 *bore doun*: 'overridden'.

726 *Nowélis*: note that the carpenter's own uneducated form is repeated in mockery of him.

727 *Thurgh fantasye, that of his vanitee*: (he was so afraid) 'through his crazy imagination, that, in his foolishness ...'

731 *par companye*: 'to keep him company'. Most of Chaucer's audience would be French-speaking, and the meaning is plain enough in any case.

732–4 *The folk gan laughen ... un-to a jape*: 'The people laughed at his delusion, and gawp and gape up into the room and made fun of all his injuries.' The slightly child-like cruelty here was probably true to life.

736–8 *It was for noght ... in al the toun*: 'It was useless, as nobody would listen to his argument; he was so talked down with impressive oaths that the whole town believed he was mad.' Oxford being quite small in those days, such an event would literally be the talk of the town.

739 *clerk*: the word reminds us of the large student population – and perhaps that the Carpenter had always been rather ready to express his distrust of learning. So all the students are happy to agree with one another, or perhaps with Nicholas, that he is mad.

And every wight gan laughen of this stryf.
Thus swyved was the carpenteres wyf,
For al his keping and his jalousye;
And Absolon hath kist hir nether yë;
And Nicholas is scalded in the toute.   745
This tale is doon, and god save al the route!

    Here endeth the Millere his tale

741   *And every wight gan laughen of this stryf*: 'And everybody laughed at this argument' (presumably the conflict of evidence, in which they all believed Nicholas's version).

742–6   *Thus swyved was ... al the route!*: 'So the Carpenter's wife was screwed, despite his jealous confinement, and Absolon has kissed her lower eye, Nicholas has been branded on the backside – the story is over, God save all this company!' The Miller sums up in a mixture of registers – 'swyve' was a fairly blunt word, for which we have no polite modern equivalent, but 'nether yë' is a shade more polite than the 'hole' he referred to earlier – perhaps, as the story comes to an end, he is aware that he is recapitulating the story for all his listeners, some of whom, like the Prioress, he might have respected for delicacy of feeling. And, of course, it might be argued that he has talked himself sober, but there has been little sign of drunkenness in his speech since he began. If the Carpenter seems to have come off badly, part of the answer may lie in the overtones of the word 'keping'. A 'keeper' came later to be a term of contempt for an old man who kept a younger woman, not necessarily his wife, and imposed unreasonable restrictions on her because of his obsessive fear of being cuckolded. The word may have some implication here.

6. Further Considerations

We began this short study of *The Miller's Tale* by asking two questions: What did this mean when it was written? What does it mean now?

Perhaps we have all come a little nearer to an answer to the first question, but we have surely realized that there can never be a complete answer to it – which does not mean that it is not an interesting and worthwhile thing to pursue. For many users of this book, a brief, wry answer to the second question may well be, 'It means I have to pass an examination on this text.' Chaucer would have found some sympathy with such a reply. In his day, examinations at the university were conducted largely by disputations, that is a sort of large oral examination in which a candidate was given some extremely abstruse point of logic or philosophy to expound in the presence of a group of scholars seeking to find flaws in his argument. The situation today is somewhat kinder.

Some 'Guides' to study include examples of typical examination questions, but we shall not do so here, still less offer 'specimen' answers for unwary students to learn off by heart and reproduce in their answers, thus giving the examiners an almost impossible task, since answers of this kind are almost always very easy to distinguish from a candidate's own thinking and writing. Instead, we might briefly consider, or reconsider, some of the ideas that have arisen in the course of these notes, and see if we can bring them together in a more concise way.

The most obvious topic for us to look at first is Chaucer's view of and way of presenting *character*. This is especially relevant to our understanding of our first question – What did it mean when it was written? – because Chaucer did not look at character quite as we do. If you are asked to give an analysis of someone's character – your own, let us say – you might say, 'Well, I'm a bit of an extrovert, but that's probably compensation for the fact that all through my adolescence I had a bit of an inferiority complex about my height ...' In a casual way we use, often not very correctly, the jargon of psychology to describe character, but that is because we live in an age that is very conscious of the existence of psychology as both an examination and an explanation of human behaviour. Some of us might use rather different terms · 'distinctly hyperthyroid – rather anaemic – a phlegmatic chap' and so on, employing terms from medicine as our means of explanation. At a rather more crude level, we might say – 'typical old School Tie – he's a real old woman –

just a punky teenage layabout,' according to our age and background. Here we are not describing characters as individuals at all, but as types. And of course many of us have met someone at a party who opens the conversation by saying, 'You have to be an Aries – I knew it as soon as you came through the door.' This is usually the prelude to a lengthy explanation of which zodiacal sign the speaker was born under and how much it has affected his or her destiny.

Of all the 'explanations' of character suggested here, the one to which Chaucer would have made the most immediate response is that including the word 'phlegmatic', closely followed by the astrological system. Like us, he had several different ways of thinking about character, and we should understand what these were in undertaking any evaluation of characterization in his work.

A very ancient system of explaining the human temperament, which goes back to early Greek medical practice and was still flourishing in Shakespeare's day and later, was that usually called 'the four humours'. The word 'humour' originally meant a fluid, a sense which survives in our word 'humid', and the belief was that there were four vital fluids in the body whose proportions determined what sort of a personality their owner would display. All diseases were attributed to a disorder of one of the humours. As one of the humours was blood, and in many illnesses the blood appears to become heated, this explains why blood-letting was such a popular medical practice – 'Wel coude he laten blood' we are told of Absolon, and a man might ask to be relieved of an ounce or two of his 'distempered' blood as we might take an aspirin.

The four fluids were blood, yellow bile or choler, black bile or choler and phlegm: blood was hot and moist, choler was hot and dry, black bile was cold and dry, phlegm was cold and moist – thus linking their properties with those of the four elements out of which it was believed everything was made – earth, air, fire and water. We can grasp the relevance of the system a little better if we realize that in contemporary English we still have four words to describe the four temperaments that these humours controlled – blood gives us the word sanguine, which we still use for an optimistic, active, outgoing character; choleric still describes someone whose emotions – especially of anger – are quickly aroused; black choler may be literally translated as 'melancholy', a word still applied to sombre, withdrawn people; and of someone who shows little emotion but goes stolidly and philosophically through life, we may say he is phlegmatic. This is very much how Chaucer saw his fellows, as falling into these categories; but, since humours were always mixed, it was normal for a person to display more than a single set of characteristics – anyone who was *always* choleric, *always* in a fury about nothing, was rather funny, and this is how the word 'humour' has come to have its modern meaning. Also the complex mixture of humours not only affected behaviour but also appearance – a melancholy person was pale, for instance – so the word 'complexion', which meant 'character' to Chaucer, has come to mean facial colouring to us.

If we apply this system to the *The Miller's Tale*, the Miller with his exuberant, quarrelsome, tipsy nature is sanguine, as is the confident Nicholas; Absolon poses as the melancholy lover, pining for his lady, but betrays some of the spite of the choleric man, whose overstressed quality we can detect in the apparently phlegmatic Carpenter. To clinch the latter's character, Chaucer describes the Reeve, on whom he is based, as 'a sclendre colerik man'.

As for Alison, she has something of a sanguine temperament, being brisk and lively enough to form a good match with Nicholas, but possibly Chaucer, if we could ask him, would say that she was born under Venus, like the Wife of Bath (who was born when Venus and Mars were in conjunction, thus giving her a bold as well as amorous disposition). The importance of Nicholas's skill in astrology was foretelling the future, but it was of equal significance in determining the outlines of an individual's life. So to Chaucer, 'character' was a combination of elements – medical (the humours) and astrological. However, he was also perfectly familiar with the 'types' we have suggested, and to some extent this is how we are to see the Carpenter – a 'typical' silly, jealous old husband, where Absolon is a 'typical' vain young man and so on.

A point of great merit in *The Miller's Tale* is that the author does not confine himself too strictly to these simple systems. Each person in the story is introduced in a slightly different way. We have noted these in passing, and now we can put them all together. The Miller himself is presented largely in a physical way, by a description of his body; but this is not only done directly, but through the use of animal imagery – the sow and fox are mentioned, and his nostrils remind us of an ape's. Also the bagpipe was an instrument associated in the medieval mind with lechery, and that is the subject of his story, indeed of most of his stories, which are described as 'harlotries'. Nicholas, the first character we are to meet, is almost wholly realized by the description of his room – we never really know what he looks like, for example. We know very well what Alison looks like, for we are told in some detail of her slim waist, her plucked, black brows and her elaborate dress – her dress, in fact, is the most detailed part of the description: but we also know what she smells and tastes like (a store of apples in hay) and what she sounds like (a swallow

tweeting away on a barn). All this tells us a good deal about what sort
of a person she was, too. Absolon's dress is also described, and here the
sense is of someone rather over-fussy in his appearance, a notion which
is confirmed by the emphasis on his crowning glory, his hair, a notorious
sign of vanity in the medieval world, who well knew the story of the
biblical Absalom, whose hair was his downfall as Absolon's silly vanity
is his. His voice, too, is important, though perhaps more important still
is his good conceit of it – he fancies himself as a serenader, and absurdly
picks a role in a Mystery play for which his light tones are quite unsuited.
John's voice we hear often when he gets going – like most chattering men
he says he is not one for talking – and the way he rambles on, repetitive,
self-opinionated and sometimes downright absurd, as in the bizarre night-
spell and his confusion of Noel and Noah, gives us a good idea of his
silliness.

It is clear that this varied way of presenting the actors is intended not
only to avoid monotony but also to affect our feelings towards them. The
'rich gnof' to whom we are introduced so abruptly at the beginning of
the story turns out to be a 'gnof' indeed, and we are not especially sorry
when his extreme jealousy and gullibility bring him a variety of misfor-
tunes. Alison and Nicholas are a well-matched, lively pair, and it is a hard
heart that begrudges them a little fun in their youth. Absolon is insuffer-
ably vain, and spiteful too, and the blast which shatters his pretensions
may well be echoed by our laughter at his folly.

We may find it less easy to laugh at the apparently blasphemous
elements in the story, some of which have been touched on in the notes
to lines 163–203 and 414–74 – the use of the Annunciation story and the
account of Noah and the Flood. It is possible, and some critics have
pursued the idea very thoroughly, to see Nicholas's seduction of Alison
as a direct parody of a scene familiar in medieval plays: the young man
represents the angel, the girl is the Virgin Mary, the seduction is carried
out primarily through the ear, which is how the Word of God was
conveyed to Mary. Whatever our religious posture, we may well feel that
this is extremely blasphemous. Medieval folk took their religion seriously
in one way – they believed very much in Hell and the Devil for instance
– but in other ways could be far more ready to joke about it (the best
'Catholic' jokes are told by Irishmen). In some of the mystery plays of the
time, highly robust humour is introduced – for example, the elderly
Joseph whose wife so mysteriously conceives is ribbed quite rudely by his
neighbours on the lines of 'Someone has left a cuckoo in your nest, Joe!'
and, if we think about it, such remarks might very well have been made

in the original situation, and the approach is realistic without being particularly irreverent.

Medieval congregations took a lively interest in preaching, too, and would have enjoyed sermons on Noah and his wicked wife. She was a favourite target for warnings about the sinful snares of the flesh – a topic always popular, as your local newsagent's stall will assure you – and also a convenient subject for attacks on women who wanted to get mixed up in men's affairs. Always on the lookout for good material to preach against the wiles of the physical, some medieval preachers even developed the story – far from the biblical account, of course – into a kind of battle between carnal temptation and righteousness. Noah's wife, a latter-day Eve, seeks to lure her husband into revealing the secrets of God. Seen from this aspect, the story becomes even more apt to Nicholas's purposes. The Carpenter's wife does obviously use her feminine wiles to help persuade him to agree to the preparations, though the carnal element is reserved for her lover.

If this all seems a long way from our own oddly ambivalent attitude to the Church, we need only remind ourselves that between us and Chaucer lies the Civil War and the imposition on the national consciousness of those Puritan values which are by no means yet defunct. Chaucer's world was probably far more deeply 'religious' than ours, but it is about the things of which we are certain that we can make jokes.

In discussing the characters and something of the religious background, we have begun to approach the moral attitude that we might adopt towards the story, and this deserves consideration, though it is a matter on which we shall not all agree, according to our age, sex and background. Chaucer wrote a number of what he called 'cherles tales' for which he briefly apologizes as a rule, and we might ask ourselves why he did so, knowing that to some they would cause offence.

First of all it should be stated that very few of his stories of this kind depend solely on improper subject-matter to be funny: they are not, that is, simply 'dirty' stories which amuse only the most childish minds. Perhaps the nearest he comes to this is in *The Summoner's Tale*, where again the bodily function of breaking wind has an important part to play. It is a fairly disgusting story, but it has a point to make – indeed, two: it is an attack on the extreme cupidity of friars, and it makes fun of medieval academic obsession with highly abstruse topics, as the Friar promised to divide what he got exactly equally amongst his brethren, and since what he got was a blast of fetid air, there follows a learned discussion of the difficulty of apportioning it.

Some such point or purpose is to be found in most of the tales of this kind: the Merchant's peculiarly nasty story of a marriage between a very old man and a young girl is interesting to set alongside the history of John and Alison – in both cases Chaucer seems to be attacking the selfish, sexual indulgence of the elderly man who is rich enough to buy what he fancies, and the Merchant merely makes the point more explicitly than the Miller. The Reeve tells a story of social pretensions bawdily brought to earth, as well as of a dishonest miller cheated so to speak in his own coin.

It is suggested that the Miller's own story has several points to make. It is an attack on gullibility. It is a satirical glance at the folly of wealthy age and lively youth trying to live together. It makes delicious fun of personal vanity and over-fastidiousness, in the fate of Absolon. Perhaps, too, it touches on a deeper matter, one on which Chaucer seems to have thought long. The social game of courtly love, with its conventions of chivalric service to your lady and its absolute rule that true love and marriage were incompatible, is the core of many of his writings. In *The Franklyn's Tale* he deliberately shows a couple who are a true love-match, and who remain 'in love' after they are married. The girl gets involved in a promise to a lover, made in an idle moment, on conditions which seem impossible, but these conditions come about and the lover claims his due. The anguish of both husband and wife as she faces her obligation to honour her word and dishonour her husband are touchingly portrayed – indeed, they touch the lover, who releases her. But there is always that feeling that anyone playing games like this is playing with fire. This is central to his lengthy treatment of the story of Troilus and Cressida, in which a lively young widow allows a man to woo and win her – but not to marry her, as she likes her freedom. When circumstances change, she feels free to take someone else to her bed, to the anguish of Troilus. Only after he is dead does he look down on this little patch of earth where he had undergone so much suffering, and see it in perspective for the folly that it was.

The Knight's Tale, which immediately precedes *The Miller's Tale*, is a picture of ideal love – love which demands nothing more than the right to love, unknown, at a distance, without hope of any kind of consummation. It is a little masterpiece on the subject – but it is not quite real. The Miller gives us earthy reality – and in Absolon, who largely apes the manners of the courtly lover, shows us that life as it is lived is not quite the same as in the poetry of high romance, whose conventions linger with us today in the cheaper kind of women's fiction by which some writers have made a very great deal of money (there is not an exact equivalent for men, but perhaps the wide provenance of 'soft' pornography is their unreality).

Chaucer was a serious man. He took his craft seriously as we have seen, here re-working a crude old story into a neat and effective narrative. The story does not condone adultery, but rather condemns mismarriage and jealousy – Nicholas gets punished, and very painfully, just as the silly husband does. In saying this, however, we should not forget what some learned editors of this text apparently never realize. Chaucer was indeed a serious author, but he had a sense of humour, and this story is, except to the prudish or the utterly unworldly, very funny. Let us heed his own conclusion –

And eek men shal nat make ernest of game.

Bibliography

There is a wealth of books about Chaucer, most of them too specialized and nearly all of them too expensive for the average student's needs or means. The simplest criterion is to find what is available from libraries.

Complete Texts
The most authoritative edition is the *Complete Works of Geoffrey Chaucer* edited by F. N. Robinson, O.U.P., 1951. This is a substantial work, but good libraries should have it. Less elaborate, but very respectable, is the complete *Chaucer* of W. W. Skeat in the Oxford Standard Authors, latest edition 1973. A modestly priced edition of the *Canterbury Tales* only, with marginal notes on difficult words, is available in the Everyman series, Dent, latest edition 1981.

The Miller's Tale
This is currently available in an edition by James Winny, published by the Cambridge University Press in 1971. It has an interesting discussion of the sources of the story in the introduction.

Modern Versions
The most popular version of the complete tales remains the 'translation' into modern verse made by Nevill Coghill, published by Penguin Books. It is lively reading, though there is some padding and modifying in order to maintain a rhyme scheme.

Background
Still available in libraries is the excellent *Chaucer* by M. W. Grose, published by Evans in 1967 – short, but full of information clearly presented.

More specialized treatment of topics we have touched on is to be found in Ian Robinson's *Chaucer's Prosody* (C.U.P., 1971), which deals at length with the problems of the verse structure; and language is examined very thoroughly in *Chaucer's English* (André Deutsch, 1974) by R. M. V. Elliott. A more recent work, V. A. Kolve's *Chaucer and the Imagery of Narrative* (Arnold, 1984), has many interesting insights and examines the first group of the tales, into which the Miller's falls, as an entity. All these books are expensive, but again should be available in good libraries.

Glossary

Most users of this book will have a text of the tale with a comprehensive glossary. However, for convenience's sake, about three hundred of the trickier words are listed here. The spelling used is that of the Skeat edition. If more than one meaning is suggested, the context will usually show which is more apt: in special cases, line numbers are given.

acordaunt agreeing with

acquitance legal document of discharge

affeccioun emotion, or perhaps fancy – see note on line 503

Almageste 'The Great Work', a famous textbook of astrology

amenden do better than, improve upon

anon at once, immediately

anon-rightes a stronger form of 'anon' – on the instant

apeiren harm, injure

art used in the general sense of learning, more particularly what would now be called science

astrelabie modern spelling astrolabe – an instrument for measuring the altitude of stars

astrologye then not distinguished from astronomy – study of the stars for divination of the future or other purposes

astromye perhaps a mistake for 'astronomye'

aswowne in a fainting fit

atones immediately

atwinne apart, separately

augrim stones counters used for arithmetical calculations

avyseth the imperative – be advised, consider

awook awoke

awroken revenged

ax/axe the first spelling is a noun, an axe, the second a verb, to ask

ayeins against

balkes the roof beams of a house

barge a larger vessel than the word now implies

barm-clooth apron

barred decorated with stripes

ben'cite! short for benedicite, God bless us!

Benedight Saint Benedict

berd beard

berne barn

bileve believe (line 348) the Creed, which begins 'I believe' in English, 'Credo' in Latin

biset used, (l. 607) literally attacked, here mistreated, maltreated

blessen to cross oneself

blosme blossom

bocler a buckler, a small round shield

bolt arrow (for a crossbow)

bord board in both modern senses
– a plank and also (l. 80)
provision for a lodger

boure(s) bedroom(s)

bragot ale sweetened with honey

brocage brokerage, the use of a
go-between

brokkinge quavering or trilling,
said of a singing voice

brosten modern 'burst' – broken

bukkes buck's – male deer, used in
a colloquial phrase (l. 279)

but often in the sense of 'unless'

cas event, (l. 553) chance

certes certainly

cetewale ginger or a similar root
spice

chartre legal document

chauncel chancel, the part of a
church where the choir sits

cherl no modern equivalent – a
low-born fellow

child (l. 217) a youth, (l. 404) child

chimenee the chimney-corner or
hearth generally

cleped named, called

clerk student, educated man
generally

cloisterer one who kept within the
cloisters, thus a monk

cokewold 'cuckold' exists as a
rather literary word – a husband
deceived by his wife

cole charcoal

colt word still used for a young
(male) horse

com pa me come and kiss me –
probably a catch-phrase

conclusioun(s) see note on l. 85;
elsewhere an agreement

conseil confidence (in the sense of
secret), (l. 422) advice

corven literally 'carved', here
incised pattern

crouche to make the sign of the
cross, to protect

crul curled

culter modern 'coulter' – the sharp
blade in front of the ploughshare

daungerous fastidious

deffye reject

demen judge

derk dark

devocioun prayers

distaf distaff, a spike on which
material for spinning is impaled

drenche drown

dreynt drowned

eek also – the word is not always
very meaningful and need not be
translated in some contexts

eft also, again

elves not the modern fairy-tale
creatures, but evil spirits

ers modern 'arse' considered
vulgar, behind

estaat condition

everichoon every-each-one,
everyone

fair not used of a colouring, but
beautiful

falding woollen cloth

falsen falsify

fanne a winnowing fan

fantasye (l. 83) interest, (l. 727) mad
idea

faste general sense of earnestly, but
at l. 391 securely, and l. 439
quickly, fast

ferde 'fared' is sometimes used, but is old-fashioned – got on, acted

fetisly neatly (of clothes), elegantly

filet a head-band to hold back the hair

forlore ruined

foyson plenty, abundance

freres friars (who travelled: monks stayed in monasteries)

froteth rubs

furlong-way a few moments

gabbe babble, chatter

gan does not always need to be translated as 'began' – test the context

gaylard lively

gentillesse courtesy – but the word implies a whole code of chivalrous behaviour

gerl young woman, l. 661 possibly in a derogatory sense – 'bit of stuff'

giterne guitar is acceptable, though the instrument we know is not quite the same

glede fire, hot coals

gnof term of contempt – ill-bred fellow

goost spirit

gore still used in dress-making – an insertion of cloth to produce a flared effect

grace favour, kindness, good fortune

grange farmhouse, perhaps simply any lonely house in the country

greyn cardamom, a spicy seed

haf past tense of heave

haliday a saint's day

hande-brede a hand's-breadth, traditionally four inches

harlotrie literally talk of prostitutes, so obscenity

harneys equipment ('harness' is misleading)

harrow! traditional cry for help

haunche-bon hip-bone

heer-aboute in this business, to do with this

heeth heather

hende epithet used throughout to describe Nicholas, perhaps ironically, as its general sense is courteous or pleasant

hente seize(d)

herkneth the imperative of hear, listen

hir her *or* their according to context

hostelrye generally a lodging house, but here not in a 'professional' sense – a house big enough to let off a room

imaginacioun fancy, fantasy

in as for 'hostelrye' above

interrogaciouns questions

jalous over-watchful, anxious rather than the modern 'jealous'

jolif gay, lively

jubbe jug

knave boy, young manservant

kyked gazed

kymelin a tub, especially for household brewing

labbe babbler, tell-tale

laten blood bleed in the sense of drain off blood for supposed medical benefit *latoun* an alloy like brass, imitation gold

laudes the first of the day services sung in monastic houses, a little before dawn – modern form, 'Lauds'

lendes thighs, including the whole area still sometimes called the loins

lewed uneducated

likerous lustful, sexy

long tall

lore advice

maistrie mastery of some skill

male bag, packet

manere kind or sort

marle-pit clay-pit

mede money offered as a gift

meeth modern mead, a drink made by fermenting honey

mete food generally

moorne yearn for

moralitee moral discussion or topic

ne common way of forming a negative of a verb – not

night-spel prayer or verse to ward off harm at night

noble gold coin

nolde contracted form of 'ne wolde' – would not

nones in the frequent Chaucerian phrase 'for the nonce' this is often meaningless: literally, 'for the occasion'

noot ne woot – don't know

note a tune – possibly the King's Note was the title of a song

offringe offertory (in church)

ordinaunce decree

out! compare *Harrow!*

paramours lovers, in a derogatory sense

pater-noster the Lord's Prayer, from its opening words in Latin

pere-jonette early pear

perled decorated with beads like pearls in shape

pigges-nye sweetie, darling

piment wine spiked with spice and sweetened with honey

pley(e) various meanings loosely connected with modern 'play' – fool about (l. 165), amuse (l. 552), joking (l. 665)

point-devys perfectly (of dress)

popelote poppet (of a girl)

Powles St Paul's (cathedral)

poyntes points, the tags, often decorative, at the ends of laces used to draw the edges of a jacket together

preche make a sermon of something

presse cupboard

privetee usual sense of private, secret, but often with a play on the sense of 'private' parts

profred offered

protestacioun public statement (*not* protest)

pryme Prime, the first service sung in daylight, between 6 and 9 a.m.

prymerole the true spelling of primrose (which is not a rose at all), hence pretty girl *purveiaunce* providence, providing for the future

queynte can be punned on: one sense is crafty or tricky, the other of a woman's vagina – the modern derivative 'cunt' is now vulgar

quinible falsetto, an artificially high voice

quod said (survived as 'quoth' in literary English)

rage fool about
rated told off, scolded
rathe early
reed advice, counsel
rente income, not only from land
rewe rue, take pity on
richesse wealth, lavishness
rometh goes
rubible small, simple kind of violin
rude uneducated

sautrye a small sort of harp
scole style, fashion
seistow do you say?
seken seek, search
sely simple (early meaning of 'silly')
sencer censer, thurible, the vessel in which incense is burned in church
sermoning (lengthy) talk
shaar ploughshare, the broad blade of the plough which turns over the furrow
shapen plan
shilde forbid (as in 'God forbid')
shode parting (of the hair)
shot-windowe a casement, window that could open and shut
sikerly certainly, surely

slye sly (person)
sloo sloe, the very dark fruit of the blackthorn
smale of physical description, slender, slim
smok (under)dress – seen note on l. 130
solas pleasure
somdeel somewhat, rather
sooth true
soster sister
spille be destroyed, die
squaymous squeamish, fastidious
stele handle: as a verb, to steal along quietly
sterte jump(ed), start(ed)
storial historical, narrative
strouted stood out
surplys white linen vestment worn over other clothes – as by modern choirboys
swelte fade away with the heat
swinke work hard, labour
swyved 'screwed' in the vulgar sense
syketh sighed

tappestere barmaid or woman publican
taverne pub
thakked felt, patted
thenche imagine, conceive
tho then
thonder-dent clap of thunder
threshfold threshold, the 'sill' of a doorway
throte throat used to mean voice
tikel chancy, uncertain
tour the Tower of London, former home of the Royal Mint
toute as for 'ers'

tow flax still in a tangled, unspun form

trave framework to hold restive horses still for shoeing

trewe generally in the modern sense of 'true' but at l. 598 faithful

trewe love a leaf of herb-paris – see note l. 584

trouthe word or promise

trowe believe

turtel a turtle-dove

underspore lever upwards from below

undertake be sure, guarantee

unnethe scarcely

upright straight in stature (l. 156), lying flat on the back (l. 336)

viritoot up and about early – see note to l. 662

vitaille (now old-fashioned) victuals – food generally

voluper head-scarf or covering

wafres modern wafers – a thin cake like a biscuit

walwinge rolling (of the motion of waves)

war 'to be war' was to know, to be aware of

wenche the word is now facetious – general sense is a girl, possibly a little derogatory: at l. 523 it means a maidservant

wende believed

wether a male (castrated) sheep

weylawey exclamation of dismay

whylom once upon a time – a formal story-opener

wightes general sense simply people – at l. 371, evil creatures

winsinge frisky

wirche to carry out

wit intelligence (no sense of funny)

wood crazy

woodnesse madness

woot know

wrighte any workman, here a carpenter

wryed twisted to one side

wyf wife or any adult woman

y-blent blinded

y-bleynt turned to one side

y-cleped called, named

y-dight decorated

yë eye (plural, 'eyen')

yeman yeoman, someone of moderate independence

yerne lively

y-forged minted (of coins)

y-grave engraved

y-herd hairy

yis colloquial form of yes

yore long ago

y-pulled plucked (of eyebrows)

y-queynt quenched (of passion)

y-wis truly, certainly

MORE ABOUT PENGUINS, PELICANS
AND PUFFINS

For further information about books available from Penguins please write to Dept EP, Penguin Books Ltd, Harmondsworth, Middlesex UB7 0DA.

In the U.S.A.: For a complete list of books available from Penguins in the United States write to Dept DG, Penguin Books, 299 Murray Hill Parkway, East Rutherford, New Jersey 07073.

In Canada: For a complete list of books available from Penguins in Canada write to Penguin Books Canada Ltd, 2801 John Street, Markham, Ontario L3R 1B4.

In Australia: For a complete list of books available from Penguins in Australia write to the Marketing Department, Penguin Books Australia Ltd, P.O. Box 257, Ringwood, Victoria 3134.

In New Zealand: For a complete list of books available from Penguins in New Zealand write to the Marketing Department, Penguin Books (N.Z.) Ltd, Private Bag, Takapuna, Auckland 9.

In India: For a complete list of books available from Penguins in India write to Penguin Overseas Ltd 706 Eros Apartments, 56 Nehru Place, New Delhi 110019.

PENGUIN REFERENCE BOOKS

☐ *Roget's Thesaurus* £2.95

Specially adapted for Penguins, Sue Lloyd's acclaimed new version of Roget s original will help you to find the right words for your purposes. 'As normal a part of an intelligent household's library as the Bible, Shakespeare and a dictionary' – *Daily Telegraph*

☐ *The Penguin Dictionary of Mathematics* £3.95

From algebra to number theory, from statistics to quantum mechanics, this new dictionary takes in all branches of pure and applied mathematics up to first-year university level.

☐ *The Penguin Dictionary of Sociology* £3.95

For students from O-level to undergraduate level, this book contains full discussions of concepts, theories and writings, with entries ranging from critical theory and behaviourism to feminism and working-class conservatism.

☐ *The Penguin Dictionary of Economics* £3.95

The third edition of this dictionary contains over 1,600 entries on economic terms and theory, the history of economics and its key individuals.

☐ *The Penguin Dictionary of Botany* £3.95

This encyclopedic reference book includes some substantial articles on vital topics as well as shorter definitions, and ranges from physiology to cell biology, microbiology to horticulture and genetics to plant pathology.

☐ *The New Penguin Dictionary of Music* £4.50

The fourth edition of this comprehensive dictionary covers orchestral, solo, choral and chamber music as well as opera and ballet, and includes detailed entries on composers, instruments of all sorts, orchestras, performers and conductors.

PENGUIN COOKERY BOOKS

☐ *Scottish Regional Recipes* **Catherine Brown** £2.95

Bridal Cake from Orkney, Chicken Stovies from the Highlands, Morayshire Apples from the North-East, Cock-a-Leekie from Edinburgh – this book of rich and satisfying recipes proves the cuisine of Scotland to be as varied as her scenery.

☐ *Jane Grigson's Fruit Book* £3.95

An alphabetical guide to fruit, packed with information and recipes. 'Not only my book of the year, but one that will have a permanent place on my shelves' – Paul Levy

☐ *Jane Grigson's Vegetable Book* £3.95

From the cabbage to the Chinese leaf, a modern kitchen guide to the cooking of vegetables by 'the most engaging food writer to emerge during the last few years' – *The Times*

☐ *Food Facts* **David Briggs and Mark Wahlqvist** £4.95

Whether you are young or old, fat or slim, fit or unwell, pregnant, or vegetarian, this lively handbook contains a comprehensive round-up of nutritional facts to help you create a satisfying diet, and live healthily.

☐ *Simple French Food* **Richard Olney** £2.95

A cookery cult, and now a classic, this book contains 'the most marvellous French food to appear in print since Elizabeth David's *French Provincial Cooking*' - *The New York Times*

☐ *Geraldene Holt's Cake Stall* £1.95

'Mouthwatering fare . . . There are scones and tea-breads, sponge and fruit cakes, family cakes, tray-baked cakes, special occasion cakes . . . Reading about them makes me feel hungry . . .' – Philippa Davenport

PENGUIN OMNIBUSES

☐ *The Penguin Complete Sherlock Holmes*
   Sir Arthur Conan Doyle   £5.95

With all fifty-six classic short stories, plus *A Study in Scarlet*, *The Sign of Four* *The Hound of the Baskervilles* and *The Valley of Fear*, this volume contains the remarkable career of Baker Street's most famous resident.

☐ *The Alexander Trilogy* **Mary Renault**   £4.95

Containing *Fire from Heaven*, *The Persian Boy* and *Funeral Games* – her re-creation of Ancient Greece acclaimed by Gore Vidal as 'one of this century's most unexpectedly original works of art'.

☐ *The Penguin Complete Novels of George Orwell*   £5.50

Containing the six novels: *Animal Farm*, *Burmese Days*, *A Clergyman's Daughter*, *Coming Up For Air*, *Keep the Aspidistra Flying* and *Nineteen Eighty-Four*.

☐ *The Penguin Essays of George Orwell*   £4.95

Famous pieces on 'The Decline of the English Murder', 'Shooting an Elephant', political issues and P. G. Wodehouse feature in this edition of forty-one essays, criticism and sketches – all classics of English prose.

☐ *The Penguin Collected Stories of*
   Isaac Bashevis Singer   £4.95

Forty-seven marvellous tales of Jewish magic, faith and exile. 'Never was the Nobel Prize more deserved . . . He belongs with the giants' – *Sunday Times*

☐ *Famous Trials* **Harry Hodge and James H. Hodge**   £3.50

From Madeleine Smith to Dr Crippen and Lord Haw-Haw, this volume contains the most sensational murder and treason trials, selected by John Mortimer from the classic Penguin Famous Trials series

PENGUIN POETRY

☐ *The Penguin Book of American Verse*
   Ed. Geoffrey Moore £5.95

'A representative anthology which will give pleasure to the general reader and at the same time presents a full range of American poetry of all periods' – *The Times Literary Supplement*

☐ *Selected Poems* **Pasternak** £2.50

Translated from the Russian by Jon Stallworthy and Peter France. 'These translations from *My Sister Life* and the other famous collections are the best we have, faithful to the originals, and true poems in their own right' – *The Times*

☐ *The Penguin Book of Bird Poetry*
   Ed. Peggy Munsterberg £3.95

'Beautifully produced and intelligently compiled. Peggy Munsterberg has done a fine job. Her anthology will please lovers of birds and of poetry alike' – *The Times Literary Supplement*

☐ *The Complete Poems* **Jonathan Swift** £10.95

A new, authoritative edition of the poems of this great satirist, pamphleteer and author of *Gulliver's Travels*. With an introduction, notes and a biographical dictionary of Swift's contemporaries by the editor, Pat Smith.

☐ *London in Verse* **Ed. Christopher Logue** £2.95

Nursery-rhymes, street cries, Shakespeare and Spike Milligan trace a route through the streets, sights and characters of London in this lively anthology, which has a linking commentary and illustrations chosen by Christopher Logue. 'A rare and delightful book' – *Country Life*

☐ *The Penguin Book of Spanish Civil War Verse*
   Ed. Valentine Cunningham £4.50

Poetry and prose making up 'an outstanding piece of historical reconstruction . . . . a human document of absorbing interest' – *The Times Literary Supplement*

PENGUIN POETRY

☐ *The Penguin Book of Women Poets*
   Ed. Cosman, Keefe and Weaver   £3.95

From Sappho and Li Ching-chao to Emily Dickinson and Anna
Akhmatova, this acclaimed anthology spans 3,500 years and forty
literary traditions; it also includes a biographical/textual note on
each poet.

☐ *Selected Poems* **William Carlos Williams**   £2.95

Poems extracted by Williams from small-town American life, 'as a
physician works upon a patient, upon the thing before him, in the
particular to discover the universal'. Edited and introduced by
Charles Tomlinson.

☐ *The Memory of War* and *Children in Exile*
   James Fenton   £2.25

Including 'A German Requiem' and several pieces on the Vietnam
War, this collection of Fenton's poems 1968–83 is a major literary
event. 'He is a magician-materialist . . . the most talented poet of his
generation' – Peter Porter in the *Observer*

☐ *Poems of Science*
   Ed. John Heath-Stubbs and Phillips Salman   £4.95

This unusual anthology traces our changing perceptions of the
universe through the eyes of the poets, from Spenser and
Shakespeare to Dannie Abse and John Updike.

☐ *East Anglia in Verse* **Ed. Angus Wilson**   £2.95

The sea, flat wheat fields and remote villages of East Anglia have
inspired poets as diverse as John Betjeman, Thomas Hood, Edward
Lear and Horace Walpole. Containing theirs and many other poems,
this is a collection 'full of small marvels' – *Guardian*

☐ *Selected Poems* **Lorca**   £2.50

With music, drama, the gypsy mythology, and the Andalusian folk-
songs of his childhood, Lorca rediscovered and infused new life into
the Spanish poetic traditions. This volume contains poems, plus
excerpts from his plays, chosen and translated by J. L. Gili.

ENGLISH AND
AMERICAN LITERATURE

☐ *Helbeck of Bannisdale* **Mrs Humphrey Ward**   £3.50

Edited by Brian Worthington. Written in 1898, a classic to rate with the novels of George Eliot and Charlotte Brontë, this is a subtle and impressive treatment of 'the love between man and woman'.

☐ *The Red Badge of Courage* **Stephen Crane**   £1.50

Introduced by Pascal Covici, Jr. 'A psychological portrayal of fear', and one of the greatest novels ever written about war: the story of a raw Union recruit during the American Civil War.

☐ *Heart of Darkness* **Joseph Conrad**   £0.95

Conrad's most profound exploration of human savagery and despair is contained in this story of Marlowe's search for Mister Kurtz in the jungle of the Belgian Congo: a vision that has haunted readers, novelists and poets throughout the century.

☐ *Selected Writings* **Samuel Johnson**   £3.95

Edited by Patrick Cruttwell. Including generous selections from his Dictionary, his edition of Shakespeare, and his *Lives of the Poets*, plus excerpts from his journalism, letters and private prayers.

☐ *Call It Sleep* **Henry Roth**   £3.50

Published in 1934, this extraordinary novel reveals, through the eyes of David Schearl (the son of immigrant Jews), a profusion of life and family relationships in the teeming jungle of a New York City slum.

☐ *A Journey to the Western Islands of Scotland*
Johnson
The Journal of a Tour to the Hebrides **Boswell**   £3.50

Edited by Peter Levi. These two journals of their joint tour of Scotland in 1773 are masterpieces of travel-writing, human observation and glorious, sardonic wit.

ENGLISH AND
AMERICAN LITERATURE

☐ *The House in Paris* **Elizabeth Bowen** £2.50

A novel that crystallizes, with delicacy and wit, the disturbing relationships between children, sex and love. 'All Miss Bowen's most brilliant qualities are here' – Jocelyn Brooke

☐ *Look Homeward, Angel* **Thomas Wolfe** £4.95

A young boy grows to manhood in small-town America. Here Wolfe displays, said F. Scott Fitzgerald, 'that flair for the extravagant and fantastic which has been an American characteristic from Irving and Poe to Dashiell Hammett'.

☐ *The Aspern Papers* and *The Turn of the Screw*
Henry James £1.95

Edited by Anthony Curtis. Containing James's two most dramatic and masterly tales: the first, a story of literary 'spoils and stratagems' set in Venice; the last, a ghost story that still puzzles the critics and terrifies all its readers.

☐ *Martin Eden* **Jack London** £2.95

Based on the author's own turbulent and legendary life, the story of a young San Franciscan seaman and his struggle to win intellectual and social recognition.

☐ *The Enlarged Devil's Dictionary* **Ambrose Bierce** £3.95

Edited by Ernest Jerome Hopkins. Containing 1,851 definitions, this spicy, satirical dictionary is for all those 'who prefer dry wines to sweet, sense to sentiment, wit to humour . . .'

☐ *The Unfortunate Traveller and Other Works*
Thomas Nashe £2.95

Edited by J. B. Steane. Sketches and writings by one of Shakespeare's most lively contemporaries: the journalist, storyteller, irreverent social critic, jester and entertainer who epitomizes the flavour and bawdy vitality of the Elizabethans.

ENGLISH AND
AMERICAN LITERATURE

☐ **_News from Nowhere_ William Morris**   £2.95

Edited by Asa Briggs. The Utopian novel, plus a selection of designs, letters, verse and writings by this brilliant artist and most unorthodox Victorian.

☐ **_Barchester Towers_ Anthony Trollope**   £1.95

Edited by Robin Gilmour. Trollope's most popular novel, and a superb comic portrayal of life and society in mid-Victorian England.

These books should be available at all good bookshops or newsagents, but if you live in the UK or the Republic of Ireland and have difficulty in getting to a bookshop, they can be ordered by post. Please indicate the titles required and fill in the form below.

NAME _____ BLOCK CAPITALS

ADDRESS _____

_____

_____

Enclose a cheque or postal order payable to The Penguin Bookshop to cover the total price of books ordered, plus 50p for postage. Readers in the Republic of Ireland should send £IR equivalent to the sterling prices, plus 67p for postage. Send to: The Penguin Bookshop, 54/56 Bridlesmith Gate, Nottingham, NG1 2GP.

You can also order by phoning (0602) 599295, and quoting your Barclaycard or Access number.

Every effort is made to ensure the accuracy of the price and availability of books at the time of going to press, but it is sometimes necessary to increase prices and in these circumstances retail prices may be shown on the covers of books which may differ from the prices shown in this list or elsewhere. This list is not an offer to supply any book.

This order service is only available to residents in the UK and the Republic of Ireland.